Architectural
PAINTING

Architectural
PAINTING

by Lawrence Grow

RIZZOLI
NEW YORK

To Martin

First published in the United States of America in 1986 by
RIZZOLI INTERNATIONAL PUBLICATIONS, INC.
97 Fifth Avenue, New York, NY 10017

Copyright © 1986 by Lawrence Grow

Book and jacket design by Frank Mahood
Composition by Typehouse of Easton, Phillipsburg, NJ
Produced by The Main Street Press, Inc., Pittstown, NJ

Printed and bound in Hong Kong

Library of Congress Cataloging-in-Publication Data
Grow, Lawrence.
  Architectural painting.

  Bibliography: p.
  Includes index.
  1. Interior decoration—United States—History—20th century—Themes,
motives. 2. Decoration and ornament—United States—History—20th
century—Themes, motives. 3. Decoration and ornament, Architectural—
United States—History—20th century—Themes, motives. I. Title.
NK2004.G76 1986   729′.4′0973   86-42708
ISBN 0-8478-0742-8

CONTENTS

PREFACE

Painters of architectural decoration are now found in all regions of North America. Ever since the 1970s, when the painting of building façades in carefully researched historical colors first became popular, the demand for the services of experienced and imaginative artists has steadily increased. The great rush to preserve and restore old buildings has been accompanied by a parallel surge in the appreciation of the extraordinary work of nineteenth and early-twentieth-century painter-decorators. Thousands of artists have been relearning the decorative techniques and finishes of the past—graining, marbleizing, glazing, ragging, trompe l'oeil, mural painting. As in any artistic renaissance, the results are mixed. There are clearly too many stencil artists now wandering country and suburban lanes tracing out totally inappropriate patterns in incongrous settings. The purpose of interior decoration—to endow and enhance architectural space with form, color, and pattern—is often misunderstood or simply overlooked.

The *raison d'être* of architectural decoration has not been overlooked in the work of the twenty artists and groups of craftsmen who are featured in the pages of *Architectural Painting*. All of these talented people have steeped themselves in the forms and finishes of the past. Whether working in a traditional or contemporary mode, or a combination of both, they successfully translate a creative tradition in painting and transform the ordinary. The group of painters chosen for this book is necessarily selective. An entire book could have been written on the traditional and postmodern work of New York-area painters alone, and a lengthy chapter could well have been devoted to the extraordinary artists of Victorian San Francisco. Rather, in order to present a true picture of the broad range of fine craftsmanship practiced today, artists from many areas have been chosen—the Far West, the Rocky Mountain states, the Midwest, the Southeast, New England, and the Middle Atlantic region. An additional listing of artists and studios is included in the closing pages of this book.

I have been greatly sustained and inspired in my work by the very artists whose work is chronicled within these pages. Not only have I been privileged to see important examples of their work, but rewarding opportunities have arisen, enabling me to discuss these projects in great detail with their creators. For special insights into this imaginative world of design, I am particularly indebted to Jeff Greene of the EverGreene Painting Studios in New York; Larry Boyce and his remarkable associates in San Francisco; the master teacher, JoAnn Day, whose workshops around the country inspire work of high quality; David Cohn and David Fisch, innovators and sensitive interpreters of the past; and Christian Thee, who understands the magic of trompe l'oeil decoration.

Without the support of my editor, Martin Greif; the careful execution of the book by Frank Mahood and John Fox; and the considerate advice of Solveig Williams of Rizzoli International Publications, the words and images on these pages would have much less meaning.

Lawrence Grow
Pinegrove
Pittstown, New Jersey
August 15, 1986

INTRODUCTION

Painted architectural decoration has existed in various forms and finishes since ancient times, its use rising and falling with changes in style and building technology. Used to define and often to enlarge space visually, architectural decoration is not mere ornamentation, a gratuitous splash of color, texture, and pattern unrelated to the overall space in which it exists. Successful architectural painting gives a façade or an interior character. Ceilings and centerpieces; wall moldings, friezes, and panels; door and window trim; floors—all of these architectural elements and many others can be enhanced, and even imitated, through the skillful application of the medium of paint.

We are living during a period of renewed interest in ornamentation. The plain boxes of post-World War II modernism are now seen for what they are—a triumph of functionalism over form. The great masterpieces of the International Style—houses designed by Phillip Johnson, Mies van der Rohe's academic buildings in Chicago, and Johnson's and Mies's triumphant Seagram Building in New York, among others—stand as exemplars of the understated, the glass and steel components combined in a dramatic manner requiring no applied decoration. Most of the imitators of the modern style, however—the commercial packagers of office blocks, apartment towers, and tract houses—did not "paint" with building materials in the style of Johnson and Mies, but opted instead for practically formless buildings stripped to only the necessities of space and light. Characterless buildings arose throughout the Western world in the years 1945-75. As space became more and more expensive and the cost of embellishing it prohibitive, design considerations took second place to economy. It is understandable, especially in crowded urban centers and in poor Third World countries, that pure and simple considerations of creating usable space should take precedence over aesthetics. A clean box is preferable to a rat-infested hovel of an ornamental era. But what we can see in our surroundings does shape our emo-

An example of the trompe l'oeil work of artist Christian Thee. The bay window and landscape—in fact, the entire scene—is a painting on a three-paneled screen. See pages 170-76.

A New York apartment living room features historic stencil designs adapted by artist Lynn Goodpasture. Peter Marino was the architect; EverGreene Painting Studios, the contractor.

tional response to daily life. Given no character, most modern spaces provide in turn no comfort, no sense of ease or security, and create a mood of boredom and indifference.

Sometime in the 1970s the tide began to turn—away from pure function to modified form in architecture. Some critics call this new type of design postmodern; others say it is simply a resurgence of ornamentalism. Yet it is more than either term suggests, and the outlines of the future in building and interior design are by no means certain. On the one hand, there is a return to pure historic forms—Victorian gables and porches, Palladian windows and broken pediment entryways of the Colonial period, the gently curved and accented walls of Art Deco—all of which are enshrined in reproduction buildings nearly identical to those of earlier periods. On the other hand, the contemporary design movement is still alive and well, practitioners of the utilitarian mixing in motifs from the past, sometimes in outrageous pastiches, but, often, with a result that extends the limits of modern design inventively and imaginatively.

The architectural painters whose collective work comprises the contents of this book, and hundreds of other practitioners of nearly ageless decorative techniques, play a very important role in both aspects of the current architectural scene—traditional and contemporary. These craftsmen have studied design history meticulously. They carefully examine the artifacts of previous decorative periods in order to properly restore or repair them. Some observers of the preservation scene may consider this labor mere copy work, but a true restoration painter always leaves something of himself behind in his work, intentionally or not. Even the finest conservators of wall murals and paintings must take some liberties with their subjects. And when replicating colors, patterns, finishes, and forms for reproduction period buildings, changes are always made along the way, even if only for compelling economic reasons rather than because of aesthetic considerations. The work done on so-called postmodern buildings allows the architectural painter an even freer hand in applying past practice, although the artist must be on guard against the tendency to introduce elements which are totally out of keeping with the established lines of the form in which they are working.

Nearly every architectural painter has begun with restoration work. Past masters of architectural ornamentation are the best teachers, and the careful study of their art is invaluable. The techniques of graining, stenciling, sponging, and gilding—and the arts of fooling the eye with trompe l'oeil painting and *faux* finishes—were almost dead by the 1970s. While the teaching of these techniques continued in various European schools, most art students in North America had no choice but to learn on the job. In the past several years, the demand for skilled craftsmen has grown so rapidly, in fact, that many people without any type of art education have become architectural painters through the expediency of trial and error. Both the academically-oriented painter and the completely self-taught have, in turn, become teachers of others, and skills which even simple nineteenth-century house painters once handed down to their apprentices are being passed along again in similar fashion.

Why, one might ask, is the work of the architectural painter of such critical interest now? His ability to endow a space with character has been acknowledged. There is, however, another fundamental consideration which has special importance in the North American setting. Skilled artists are able to give something most of us can no longer afford. They create illusions—make-believe marble, mahogany, gold, malachite, even such common materials as brick and slate. Through the art of trompe l'oeil painting, they visually expand space beyond its physical limits. Existing crown moldings, panels, wainscoting, and various types of trim may be painted in a manner that enhances their value and appeal. But more important, the skilled artisan can *simulate* such elements through the use of paint alone. The houses of early America are often decorated with such artistic ''fakery.'' Few colonists could afford elaborate millwork, fancy imported wallpapers, or luxurious marble, and they turned to painter-decorators to brighten their homes. The affordability and availability of special materials are nearly as limited now as they were 200 years ago. Besides, the *faux* has an appearance all its own, qualities of artistic merit nearly as valuable as the real thing. Painted finishes, artist JoAnne Day explains, are meant ''to fool the eye and yet still look *faux*, a trick that requires skill and imagination.''

It is this combination of skill and imagination that is celebrated in the pages of *Architectural Painting*. In twenty illustrated chapters, the delightful, often surprising, and always engaging artwork of a new generation of American artisans comes very much alive.

A documentary photograph used by Designed Communications in re-creating original paint textures for the ceiling of the Lafayette Building in Little Rock, Arkansas. See pages 40-47.

Architectural
PAINTING

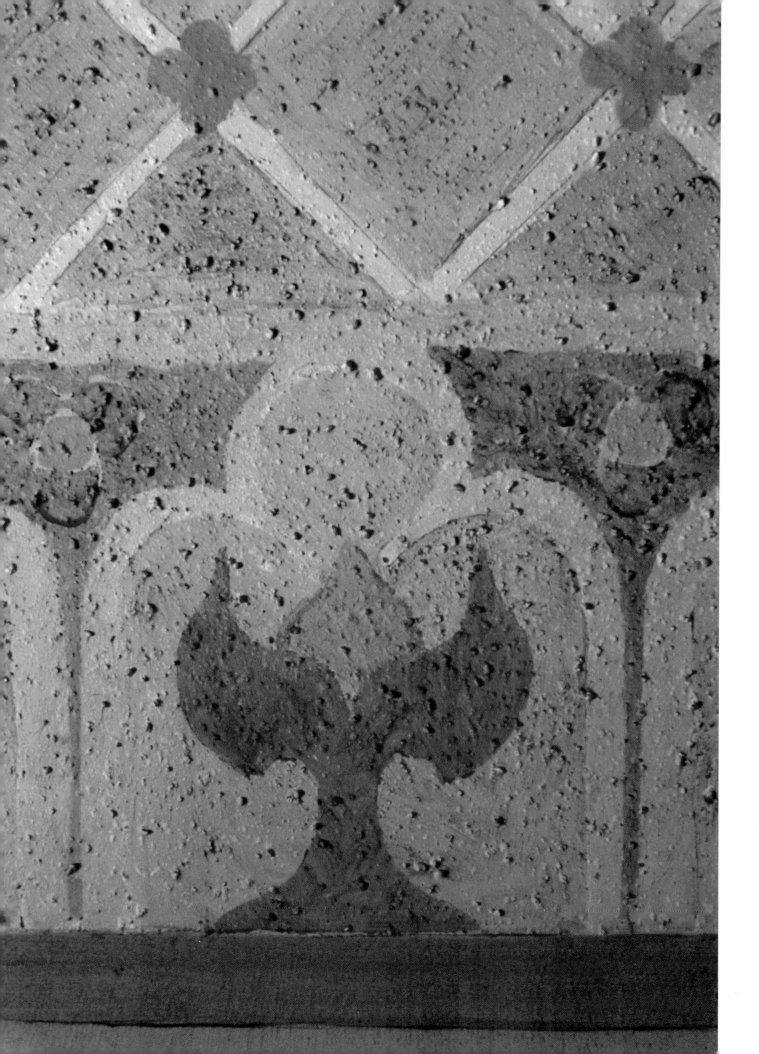

Learning from the Past

Like many American decorative painters of the 1980s, Scott Waterman mastered his skills on the job. Before the advent of the postmodernists, there was little place for an ornamental artist in the stylish world of twentieth-century architecture and interior design. And formal training in the fundamental techniques of altering flat surfaces did not form a part of the design school curriculum for students. Restoration of existing ornamental surfaces—repainting and gilding ceilings and walls— provided the only outlet for artistic training for Waterman and his contemporaries. But in retracing the lines of the past, a lost art was recovered and invigorated. Fortunately, after graduation from the Atlanta College of Art in 1979, Waterman became involved in the restoration of Atlanta's Moorish fantasy movie palace, the 1929 Fox Theater. This ongoing project has engaged the talents of many crafts people; the re-creation of the ornamentation of the Arabian nights will require many years of exacting copy work. From time to time, Waterman returns to the scene of his apprenticeship to contribute something more to this admirable restoration. He has absorbed enough from it, however, to have moved on to other restorations and to new work which incorporates the techniques and the appeal of the old.

A detail from a tray ceiling in an Atlanta residence is striking evidence of Waterman's imaginative rendering of flat surfaces. Stenciling and free-hand painting have been utilized in this adaptation of a design based on the interior decoration of a chapel by Viollet-le-Duc.

A rough plastered surface serves as the base for the artwork. Transparent oil glazes accentuate the soft mosaic appearance and give the design a depth and definition lacking in the usual flat surface.

The interior of a French provincial residence in the Atlanta suburbs, completed in 1985, has the look of another time and place. Scott Waterman painstakingly created *faux* finishes which capture the comfortable patina of age and elegance. At the same time, he has carefully avoided a period look, the sterile copying of an antique interior. His painted effects are both pleasing and entertaining.

The fireplace wall has been roughly stuccoed to simulate the weathering effects of time. A mottled glaze, applied to those areas free of intentional distress, and the smoky stain issuing from the hearth produce a theatrical illusion of age.

The paneled oak cabinets and cupboards have a soft, sun-bleached appearance— the result of polychrome decoration, staining, and distressing.

A set of French provincial chairs has been decorated in the same gray palette as the surrounding kitchen cabinets.

From the ceiling—glazed to give the effect of water staining—to the rough-textured stone floor, Waterman has successfully combined a series of *faux* finishes. Even the dishwater and refrigerator/freezer are incorporated in the decorative scheme.

The simplest elements in a country interior can be brought alive with light decorative touches. The beams and trusses, shown before and after ornamentation, were first stained a driftwood gray, then naively stenciled, and finally wiped with primary pigments. The effect is both charming and fitting.

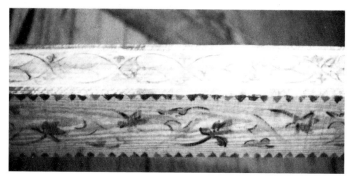

What can one do with an oddly-shaped attic room? Scott Waterman chose to open up the ceiling to the sky. The trompe l'oeil bamboo lattice design is based upon a classic Chinese pattern. From the lattice trail garlands of wandering nasturtium and morning glory vines. The painted doors leading into this outlandish attic garden room are decorated with designs of the type made fashionable in English country houses of the 1930s by Vanessa Bell and Duncan Grant.

The Ponce apartment building, built in the 1910s near Atlanta's center, suffered many indignities until it was restored in 1983. The soaring lobby had lost some of its *scagliola* or imitation marble decoration, and the varied surfaces and elements required total reworking. Waterman and former partner Janet West stenciled, hand-painted, gilded, and glazed the entire space over a three-month period. Waterman is shown at right painting one of the columns.

The cove was hand-stenciled and then finished with a transparent glaze. The gold of the design harmonizes with the gilt of the brackets and moldings. Successful gilding of these surfaces and other three-dimensional architectural elements in the lobby required an especially firm hand and patient demeanor. Although only accents in the overall design of the space, these gilt borders define the various levels of decoration.

Other key elements in the restoration of the Ponce lobby included stenciling of a wall festoon, glazing and gilding of coffered ceiling areas, and hand-painting of capitals, columns, and pilasters.

Each of the elements in the coffered ceiling was painted and gilded. The stenciled festoon design was also gilded.

All of the capitals were polychromed after the decorative work had been repaired.

The pilaster has been stenciled and hand-painted.

Small spaces are often those which profit the most from the skill of the decorative painter. The anteroom of Trotter's Restaurant in Atlanta was visually enlarged and enriched with such trompe l'oeil effects as simulated leather-upholstered walls and pilasters. The dusty rose color imitates that found in the restaurant's authentic upholstered furniture.

"Tricks Requiring Skill and Imagination"

At the turn of every century," says artist JoAnne Day, "people look to the past to preserve and restore, as well as inspire, the design of the future." The late Victorians, for example, abandoned the Gothic arch in the 1880s and embraced the elegant lines of the Colonial Revival. As the fin-de-siècle of the modern age approaches ever closer, our aesthetic clocks are also being turned back—to the Belle Epoque of 1900, to the Art Deco of the 1930s, to the two-toned streamlining of the 1940s and '50s. Nostalgia grows deeper; romanticism returns, and this is good news for the ornamentalists who have revived the craft of decorative painting. JoAnne Day was one of the first new masters of the *faux* finish. Although raised and trained in the New York area during the 1960s and early '70s, she established her reputation and The Day Studio-Workshop in San Francisco in 1975. From that base she and her associates have fanned out across the country with a series of seminars and workshops in wall glazing and painted finish techniques. Hundreds of new painters have been taught the fundamental steps in distressing, glazing, pickling, marbleizing, graining, and trompe l'oeil work.

The projects directed by JoAnne Day illustrate her talent as an imaginative colorist and special effects designer. The Bank of Los Angeles branch at the corner of La Cienega and Santa Monica Boulevards, with its seeming jade columns, and the newest and exotic Banana Republic outlet on New York's East Side are complex, multilayered creations of painted finishes. Samantha's restaurant, carved out of a nondescript contemporary San Francisco building on Levi's Plaza, also displays how a conventional interior can be made interesting. In three-and-a-half days during 1985, Day and a team of five assistants succeeded in transforming a modern box into a restaurant which might have existed before San Francisco was jolted by the earthquake of 1906. This transformation was accomplished almost entirely by the use of painted finishes on surfaces meant, as Day explains, "to fool the eye and yet still look *faux*, a trick that requires skill and imagination."

An enclosed glass arcade serves as the entrance and one of four dining areas in Samantha's restaurant owned by Sam Duvall of the Cafe Ritz in Los Angeles and New York. The formal elegance of the façade is heightened by the marbleized treatment of the window segments and planter boxes.

JoAnne Day had full control of the design and decoration of Samantha's, a luxury not enjoyed by most decorative painters on similar commercial projects. Having the final say on the choice of fabrics and other materials as well as the mode of lighting has resulted in an unusually well-integrated design.

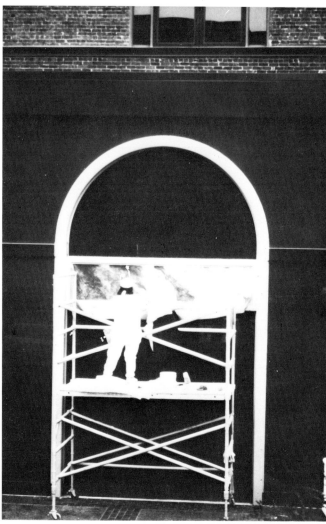

Marbleizing of each exterior panel and planter was done in exterior oils on plywood. An overglaze was then applied over the finish and the panel was urethaned.

Much of the interior wall space was glazed with a preparatory oil coat and then finished with a deeper color to give the patina of age.

The dado is composed of marbleized panels like those of the upper walls. These are set against a glazed field. Marbleizing a surface is sometimes referred to by its English term, *scumbling*. The opaque glaze most often used can also be known as a *scumble* or *scumble glaze*.

A corner of Samantha's Beauregard Room shows to what extent the designer succeeded in creating a salon of the early 1900s. Decoration of the columnar flower stands is shown on p. 30.

The main dining room and bar are enriched by the addition of mahogany paneling and dividers. Metal casings used here were grained to blend in with the wood without detection. The new wood floors were distressed to produce a warm antique finish.

Columns used for holding containers of cut flowers are as false and fitting as the marbleized wall panels. The dark color blends well with similarly treated baseboards and the pink-gray "marble" of the walls.

The finish for an irregular architectural element may require several glazes to produce depth and pattern. Additional lustre and protection can come from the application of a varnish.

The bar was completely refinished to match the other elements in the main dining room.

Soft and unobtrusive paint finishes provide a restful atmosphere in the main dining room. The sensibility expressed is of a fine private space and not a jarring commercial interior.

Celebrating the Unconventional

David Fisch likes to tackle the difficult—rooms with few architectural elements and almost inaccessible spaces. Working out of an old Dutch Colonial stone house on the New York-New Jersey border that will require years of restoration work, the artist converses knowledgeably of Pompeii and its faded glories, postmodern architecture, and "environmental rooms." Schooled in the fine and liberal arts at the University of Chicago during the late '60s, and raised in a home where politics and aesthetics were daily staples, Fisch celebrates the unconventional. He speaks of his imaginative proposal to decorate the ceiling of the catalog card room at the New York Public Library, of his work for designer John Saladino, of his appreciation for the effects of time on surfaces. Like many of his contemporaries, Fisch is both an antiquarian and a visionary, digging into the past for inspiration and interpreting his finds in new and engaging ways. At age 36, he has already received recognition from such influential publications as *The New York Times* and *House &*

Garden. Yet he tires quickly of the trendy and fashionable, always seeking out novel approaches that will liberate dull space from the flat plane and imbue it with meaning.

Few interior spaces are more dull in character and difficult to design than the modern bathroom. For inspiration, Fisch turned to the ruins of Pompeii for the decorative detail. The ceiling was vaulted to receive a trompe l'oeil coffered design. All the wall painting was executed on canvas so that it could be removed if necessary. His treatment intentionally incorporates the weathering effects of time, a playful reminder that time is as much an imaginative dimension as it is a verifiable state.

Working only on canvas with oil paints, David Fisch has transformed a characterless space into an intriguing and delightful sanctuary.

Jeff Blechman

A studded door reminiscent of a medieval portcullis is, in reality, only a flat painted surface. Such decorative anachronisms appear in many of the nearly forty projects which Fisch has completed since 1978. His love of mixing visual references to the past in modern spaces has drawn the attention of like-minded postmodern designers and architects.

Jeff Blechman

Jeff Blechman

35

Fisch intended that anyone entering this front hall should feel as if he were walking into the midst of a drawing. Trompe l'oeil effects are subtle and deceiving. The ornamental swag over the green door is cast iron painted to look flat; that over the paneled door is trompe l'oeil. Marble and plaster were combined to form the basin and painted to look like scalloped lead. Soft lighting directs the eye upward to the vaulted ceiling which is decorated with classical motifs and finished to resemble antique mosaic work. Fisch completed this project for New York designer John Saladino in 1984.

Fisch continued his visual tricks in the richly decorated foyer by painting shadows across the trompe l'oeil ceiling and the walls. This creates the illusion of a strong light source above.

The main hall of a New York apartment on Riverside Drive has been decorated in a manner calculated to deceive the eye. From surface appearances, there appear to be two openings at one end, that on the left leading into a living room with a view of the Hudson and the other opening up to the entryway. The perspective of the recessed painting at the left is so composed as to truly fool the senses.

A series of paintings depicting the four seasons was executed by Fisch in the atrium of John and Virginia Saladino's Connecticut country house. These are painted on canvassed walls. Framed in a false doorway is "Autumn." "Winter," "Spring," and "Summer," clockwise from upper left, respectively, define other sides of the space. The overall design of the room is suggested by Pompeiian models.

Re-creating the Historical Record

The historic preservation movement of the 1970s and '80s has brought about a revival of interest in the decorative techniques and designs of Colonial and Victorian craftsmen. Responding to the need for skilled artisans who can restore or re-create period decor, many individuals in North America and Europe have taught themselves the fundamentals of decorative painting. The first steps in this educational process were often small ones, perhaps involving a simple stencil frieze or a festoon for the living room of a friend's house. Suzanne Kittrell and Rebecca Witsell, partners in Designed Communications of Little Rock, Arkansas, started out in this manner in the mid-'70s. Ten years later, having graduated to much larger and complex projects, they enjoy an enviable professional reputation.

Kittrell and Witsell have mastered the process of documenting a project before it is executed, a step especially necessary when time and neglect have almost completely obscured the visual record. Providing a valid historical base from which to proceed with redecoration, they explain, requires careful analysis of remaining colors and patterns as well as a study of the techniques used in achieving them. In addition, the decorative painter must possess a thorough knowledge of any period style in which he is called to work. Adaptation of an original design may be required. In such a case, necessity will truly be the mother of invention, but the adaptation will still have to be of the same character as the original.

Challenges such as these delight Kittrell and Witsell. Their book, *Authentic Stencil Patterns: 1890-1930,* a compilation of designs found by them in the actual catalogs used by professionals to order hand-cut stencils, is now widely used by other artisans in the United States. The important commissions Designed Communications has successfully completed—the Lafayette Building and the Belle Tournure complex in Little Rock being of special note—offer striking testimony to the skill with which Kittrell and Witsell reveal and interpret the past.

The decoration of the Lafayette Building lobby, formerly a hotel, was restored in 1984 by a Designed Communications team of six.

Wesley Hitt

When it opened in 1925, the Lafayette Hotel was one of Little Rock's showplaces. The lobby of the ten-story building—a handsome interplay of varnished red gum paneling, grained and stenciled beams, and a polished marble floor—was designed to impress guests of every rank. Closed for a time during the Depression, it opened again in the early 1940s and this is when the ceiling was last decorated.

Witsell, Evans & Rasco P.A.

The building was restored and adapted for use as a luxury office center by American Diversified Capital Corporation of Costa Mesa, California. Baldwin & Shell Construction Co. was the general contractor, and Witsell Evans & Rasco P.A., the architects and planners.

Witsell, Evans & Rasco P.A.

The striking designs of the plaster ceiling beams had been completely painted over by the time Designed Communications was called in to restore them in 1984. Layers of paint were carefully stripped away to reveal something of the original design.

Witsell, Evans & Rasco P.A.

Before beginning their work, Kittrell and Witsell researched the career of the last decorator of the hotel lobby—John Oehrlie, a Swiss mural painter. In this photograph (c. 1940), he is shown to the right painting one of the hundreds of designs incorporated in the ceiling. Chief decorator of the Southwest Hotels chain that owned the Lafayette, Oehrlie often worked with his son-in-law, shown at left.

Overleaf: A documentary photograph of the 1940s design taken after the beams had been stripped. The redecoration was executed in the same style shown—brown line stencil designs were drawn and filled in with glazes on the undersides; the sides were grained.

1

5

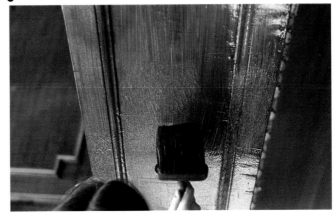

2

The project called for (1) the application of brown line stencil designs, (2) painting of brown connecting lines, (3) hand-painting of some of the patterns, or (4) stenciling of other colored shapes. Glazes were then hand-applied, wiped, and softened with cheesecloth. Finally, (5) the sides of the beams were grained with a flogger. The distribution of the colors is shown in (6), an in-progress photograph.

3

6

4

46

New commercial buildings built for retailers serving a fashionable clientele are today more luxurious in appointments than they have been for many years. Belle Tournure, built in 1985 in Little Rock, is an exclusive women's shop featuring designer clothing, a French restaurant, and a beauty salon. Designed Communications executed the decorative details which lend the various spaces their elegant character. Lawson, Gentry Interiors of Little Rock designed the interiors.

Wesley Hitt

The work performed by Suzanne Kittrell and Becky Witsell, assisted by artist Kathy Worthen, included marbleizing, trompe l'oeil, and various types of *faux* finishes. The main sales floor is distinguished by handsomely marbleized columns in a *faux* Rojo Alicante finish. The elevator shaft facades and doors are decorated in the same fashion, with the doors also carrying a trompe l'oeil design simulating carving.

Above a limestone mantel perches a monkey playing a flute. It is all an illusion, of course, as the simian musician sits only in a trompe l'oeil niche. The finish of the overmantel is *faux* limestone.

Wesley Hitt

Wesley Hitt

The reddish-brown columns and pilasters, veined in white, form an elegant entryway to the main dining area of the restaurant. They are among thirty-seven marbleized in this manner. The high satin finish was achieved by the application of several layers of varnish.

A Caravan of Peddling Painters

When Larry Boyce first began his professional career in the 1970s, he traveled by bicycle from project to project in the San Francisco area. Paints, brushes, stencils, and antique pattern books were stuffed in a backpack; a sleeping bag and personal effects were slung across the bicycle frame. Boyce became a well-known figure on the avenues of the Bay area, and gradually his journeys became longer and longer, reaching out to other California communities and to towns in the Pacific Northwest and the Rocky Mountain states. Often he would spend two weeks or even a month camping out in the home or office of a patron, working most of the day and night on a complicated ceiling design. Painting ceilings became his passion, and demand for his services became so great that assistance was necessary. This was no problem for Boyce had already attracted talented followers to his art and itinerant lifestyle. Thus was born Larry Boyce & Associates, a caravan of peddling painters who, over the past three and a half years, have tackled such diverse projects as a synagogue, the Beverly Hills home of a movie star, a bed and breakfast inn, and a Portland, Oregon, hotel. Now, in

association with EverGreene Painting Studios (see pages 94-107), Boyce & Associates is at work on the office of the Vice President of the United States in Washington's landmark Executive Office Building, restoring the extraordinary painted decoration of the 1870s. From this office they will soon move on to others in the multi-tiered Second Empire complex.

Now that they have reached the pinnacle of professional success, Boyce and his associates do express some concern about being able to tackle as many projects as they would like. Yet, even as the work in

The walls and ceiling of a room used solely for meditation in a private San Francisco residence were elaborately stenciled and gold-leafed by Boyce & Associates. Tom Ciesla is shown stenciling the ceiling, using a template that can be moved from one position to another.

Washington continues, they are painting and restoring ceilings and walls elsewhere. The jobs they undertake are usually so ambitious in scope and costly in time and materials that work has to proceed in various stages. Restoration work on the seventy-year-old stenciled ceiling of the San Francisco temple, for example, will require a number of years to complete. The necessary scaffolding is left in place when time and the congregation's budget will allow work to recommence.

One or two members of the group are always working

Larry Boyce describes the decoration of the meditation room as a free interpretation of Italian Renaissance design with the addition of Roman and Greek motifs. The segmental division of wall space, however, was chosen because of the lines of the room's bay window to one side. Arches, lunettes, and spandrels repeat the basic window profile and give to the boxy space a definite design character. Dramatic use has been made of the heavy crown molding, picture molding, and high ceiling emblazoned with a center rosette.

Before any stenciling work was done, the various segments were painted in a palette of blue and rose, tones chosen for their luminescent and close value. Gold leaf was then applied to the moldings and used to outline the arches.

out of the San Francisco area. It is here that some of Boyce & Associates' most original projects have been completed. Slightly off-beat by the traditional standards of architectural preservationists, these are rooms decorated in a highly ornate, eclectic fashion. The sten-

ciled ceiling and walls of the meditation room in the Gatewood residence, completed in 1984, required the work of all the associates. It is a room in which their technical skill and aesthetic sensibility are fully visible.

All of the decorative motifs were stencil-painted, a method simple in theory but requiring an expert hand in practice. The task of decorating the meditation room was made more difficult by the layering of one design over another, especially on the ceiling. More than 2,000 hours were spent painting the room.

Acrylic paints were used throughout because of their ability, in Boyce's words, "to assume a completely matte appearance which disguises individual brush strokes and texture." For the major frieze panel design, Boyce adapted the work of P.B. White, a prominent nineteenth-century architect and painter.

Many nineteenth-century homes now appear more interesting and pleasing in decor because of the restoration work performed by Boyce & Associates. Architectural detailing such as moldings, casings, ceiling rosettes, and wainscoting is delineated in colors and patterns which emphasize the character of the space.

The front parlor of a private mid-nineteenth-century residence has a large and high expanse of ceiling and an imposing crown molding. Stencil designs, floral papers, gilt, and glazed finishes are used to give the room the handsome, well-defined appearance typical of the period. The reproduction frieze paper, in a gold pattern, and the ceiling paper, a dusty multicolor design, are both from Bradbury and Bradbury of Benicia, California. Gilt is used to delineate the picture molding and elements of the crown molding. Further interest is created in the ceiling by segmenting the border space with several different stencil patterns. A stenciled pattern of trailing ivy also decorates the crown molding.

Chad Slattery

Chad Slattery

A front hall should be an inviting place. Often it is a narrow, dark, and unattractive space. Boyce and Associates have emphasized the best features of the hall through graining, stencil painting, glazing, and gilding. The walls are a soft, mottled blue-green which blends handsomely with the rich brown of the doors and the Lincrusta-Walton wainscoting. The crown molding is gilded and painted, as is the ceiling rosette. Stenciled patterns decorate the ceiling.

Chad Slattery

Chad Slattery

Chad Slattery

Chad Slattery

Mastering the Art of Ornamentation

Owen Jones's *Grammar of Ornament*, first published in 1856, has influenced many generations of decorative painters in North America. Designs of the Islamic and Hispanic worlds were the primary interest of the English designer, architect, and writer, but in his classic work he also articulated the principles of good craftsmanship and honesty in the use of materials, precepts which guide architectural painters today as they did in the Victorian era. Ken Miller and Larry Lyons, partners in The Grammar of Ornament, Inc., of Denver, carry on Jones's tradition in name and in deed. Self-taught painters and restoration craftsmen, they have meticulously examined the work of past masters and evolved into artists who not only copy what was done in the past but who also make original contributions. In their work, Miller and Lyons shuttle between Victorian historicism, examples of which abound in Colorado's boom towns settled in the nineteenth century, and postmodern ornamentalism. Since the firm's founding in 1977, commissions have included the restoration of the Grand Hallway ceiling of the United States Mint in Denver, a project which, unfortunately, cannot be photographed because of Treasury Department regulations; the Wheeler Opera House in Aspen; a Denver piano lounge,

and numerous private homes. In each of these projects, Miller and Lyons have demonstrated technical expertise and an inspired way with color and pattern.

The opera house ceiling was painted a rich deep blue which blends well with the cherry wood graining of the opera box, here shown partially complete. A lighter oak finish was used for other paneling.

Larry Lyons is shown gilding a decorative panel, one of seven ornamenting a box in Aspen's Wheeler Opera House. Lyons and Ken Miller also grained and gilded the auditorium's ceiling beams, proscenium, and wainscoting. Stenciling, striping, and gilding were executed in portions of the coves, ceiling, and stage.

The dining room ceiling in a private home was glazed in a gray-silver shade and stenciled with an oriental motif against a blue field. At the ceiling's center is a rosette design adapted from an oriental carpet motif in grays, blues, and touches of red.

An Eastlake front parlor has been handsomely finished with a simple gold crown molding and, above it, several bands of stenciled designs in green, beige-pink, and brown. The plaster ceiling rosette has been painted to highlight its ornate lines.

The oldest remaining single-family dwelling left in downtown Denver has undergone considerable restoration work and has been adapted successfully for law offices. Stencil designs appear in several of the rooms and are representative of late-nineteenth-century taste. Illustrated is a frieze design of repeated small figures worked in gold and brown. The high ceiling is outlined in a simple stencil pattern.

The colorful stencil designs used on the walls and ceiling of the library in a private Denver home are wonderfully evocative of the Victorian passion for ornamentation. Other than the doors and casings, the room is bare of architectural detail. The Grammar of Ornament team has used this absence to great advantage, segmenting the beige walls with bands of complementary blue, red, and gold designs. The repetition of the checkered motif on the ceiling draws the space together, the deep red expanse of the dado providing a handsome base.

In the late-Victorian period a slate or cast-iron mantel was often installed in place of a more expensive marble one. Naturally, the Victorians chose to marbleize such base materials, to render them more elegant. The Grammar of Ornament has restored a number of cast-iron mantels, including such small details as the *faux* incising of the panels.

The Victorian love of combining various types of ornamental materials in one room is fully illustrated in this dining room. The cornice is wood-grained in a dark shade of brown; below it is a stenciled frieze in an Anglo-Japanese pattern. Embossed paper—Anaglypta—is used in place of a true Japanese leather paper to fill the space between the picture rail and the chair rail. Traditional stencil patterns decorate the dado.

Ivory's, a Denver piano bar lounge, was designed and executed by Miller and Lyons in an Art Moderne style of curved lines and geometric patterns. The wall paintings, mirror, fireplace, and wainscoting designs are original to the project. Mahogany and metallic trim is used for the wainscoting. The baseboard has been marbleized to match the fireplace.

To the New York Manner Born

If it were not for the fact that Nancy Kintisch is an inveterate New Yorker, she might be spending all of her time on the West Coast designing and executing sets for Hollywood fantasies. Although Kintisch works at least several weeks in California each year, she is most at home in the fast-paced world of New York merchandising and interior design. It, too, is a fantasy world of visual exaggeration, of escapism and unreal expectations. She thrives on the commercial, on the intentionally kitsch. Conversing with her in a glitzy diner along Tenth Avenue in midtown Manhattan, there is no surprise in learning that Kintisch has designed the popcorn stand at the Ziegfeld Theater, decorated a Regency Hotel ballroom, provided visual effects for a trendy clothing store on the lower East Side, and, between trips to Beverly Hills to paint Bette Midler's house, is creating props to be used in a Bloomingdale's catalog. She loves it all, but the work that is most satisfying is the most painterly—Midler's New York apartment and a foyer painted in the style of Henri Rousseau. Kintisch is first and foremost a painter and holds a B.F.A. degree from the Rhode Island School of Design. Architectural painting allows her to paint on a large scale, she explains, and to employ illusionary effects in a living environment.

The foyer of a Manhattan apartment has been completely transformed into a jungle setting. Only the necessary door hardware remains untouched, the peephole having been converted into an all-seeing eye. Kintisch often signs her work as she has here in the lower left of the color illustration.

Kintisch has collaborated on completely unorthodox projects with equally talented designers such as Michael Formica and Alan Buchsbaum. The foyer painted to look like an elevator interior was designed by Formica. It matches almost exactly the decor of the cab in which one rides to reach the apartment foyer.

Other than the real elevator door, only three items in the foyer are real—the detection mirror, fan, and overhead light. *Faux bois* painting of various types simulates the elevator woods.

Everything was designed and executed to amaze and delight anyone entering the foyer from the elevator for the first time. From all appearances, even the control panel, inspection certificate, manufacturer's plate, and call panel are as real as their models. The exact replication through trompe l'oeil painting also extends to the air vents in the wall and the porthole of the entry door to the apartment.

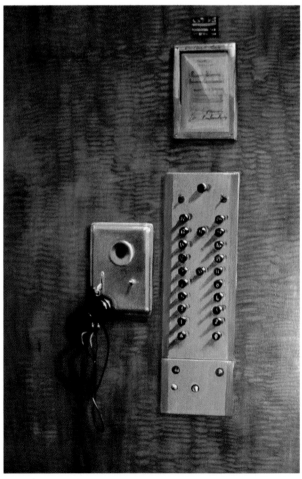

Architect Alan Buchsbaum designed a loft apartment in an old New York warehouse and carved a small vestibule out of open space near the tenant-operated freight elevator. Nancy Kintisch executed the unusual design as if it had been set into wet cement or plaster. The walls are painted to appear as if they contain mosaic tiles and incised patterns. The elevator doors are painted in a design inspired by Gustav Klimt, a favorite artist of the loft's owner.

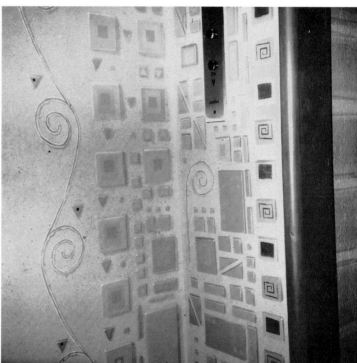

Michael Formica designed the apartment decorated in what he and Nancy Kintisch describe, tongue-in-cheek, as the "Louie-Louie" style. Three shades of gray were used by Kintisch to paint the mock French period decoration. Other areas were marbleized to suggest columns.

Following in the Itinerant Tradition

David Bradstreet Wiggins bears a name that suggests his New England patrimony. In conversation, the self-taught painter conveys a sober but spiritual attitude toward life and work which places him very much in the tradition of his Calvinist forebears. Born during World War II, he has lived most of his life as an itinerant mural painter, traveling from home to home in the same manner as such early nineteenth-century artists as Rufus Porter, Moses Eaton, and John Avery. Their naive folk paintings have always fascinated Wiggins. Similarly, the visionary work of Erastus Salisbury Field has been of influence. The unusual combination of innocence and untutored sophistication intrigues Wiggins. "The fact is that the folk artist has filled much more than just the dark interiors of New England homes" he explains. And so, too, does Wiggins. His murals are sweeping panoramas of a metaphysical early America, landscapes dotted with imaginary ruins and the symbolic commonplace.

One of Wiggins's most recent works is the seven-panel mural entitled "That Ancient City from Whose Bourne No Traveler Ever Returned." The title is a paraphrase from Shakespeare's *Hamlet* and refers to the finality of death. Painted on wooden door panels in which the open grain is subtly visible, the mural possesses an atmospheric intensity of color and a magical flow of line.

While most of Wiggins' murals are painted directly on the walls of his patrons' homes, he is now turning to the use of canvas so that he can work out of his Tilton, New Hampshire, studio. The mural on canvas in progress is untitled and is based on an Old Testament theme.

The mural in the front parlor of an early nineteenth-century Connecticut house is a recent commission which required on-the-spot attention over a period of several weeks.

Wiggins has also painted the interiors of contemporary buildings, including the headquarters of the Timberpeg corporation in Hanover, New Hampshire.

One of the sections of the artist's seven-panel mural.

Old World, New World

I t seems most appropriate that Granada Hills in the sun-drenched "Valley" of Los Angeles County should now be the home of Hellmut and Hellgah Dieken. Accomplished painters of fantasy scenes and vignettes, the German couple is naturally drawn to the lifestyle of southern California, to the type of grand gestures in interior design and architecture found in the homes and watering places of international café society. Born before World War II in the shadow of Cologne's most dramatic and decorative landmark, the high-Gothic cathedral, both Hellmut and Hellgah mastered the fine art of mural painting during the 1960s in the design schools and studios of Germany and France. Unlike most contemporary American architectural painters, the Diekens did not discover their calling by accident when restoring the work of another generation of artists, but were formally trained in their métier. The Diekens *are* of another generation professionally, one that never disappeared in Europe but continued the ornamental tradition in the face of modernism. Their artistic credits from Munich,

Paris, Monaco, Berlin, Vienna, and elsewhere in central Europe read like a page from an international edition of *Vogue* — the Hotel Kempinski in Berlin and Monte Carlo's Hotel Paris; assignments from publisher Axel Springer and coffee magnate Walther Jacobs; work for the Princess Anne Marie von Bismarck and Princess Johanna zu Sayn-Wittgenstein.

The Diekens came to the United States in 1982, first settling in a twenty-room version of a European castle in Greenwich, Connecticut. It was from here that they undertook the design of the first model apartment in New York's Trump Tower. As illustrated on the following pages, it is rich in classical allusion and makes effective use of trompe l'oeil effects. The artists' West Coast commissions, undertaken since 1984, exhibit a similar mastery of perspective, architectural detail, and playful imagery drawn from classical art. In this period of postmodern expression, their work does constitute, as the Diekens explain, "art designs for our times."

The patio of a Bel Air, California home, completed in 1984, has a striking Roman character. It is a perfect setting for the stenciled and hand-painted wall murals and their timeless classical and geometric designs. The trompe l'oeil painting of the mural portico adds a fantastic dimension to what could well be a Hollywood set. The real columns have been marbleized and decorated in the same warm, earth-toned palette as the interior space.

The Diekens are equally at home in the grand manner of eighteenth-century French painter-decorators. In this pavilion of a Greenwich, Connecticut, home, trompe l'oeil moldings surround a hand-painted ceiling mural executed in oil on canvas.

Almost as much time is spent by the Diekens in sketching out their plans as in the execution of them. The Bel Air project was swiftly completed in several weeks once the basic architectural forms were in place. As a comparison between the drawing and a photograph of a completed section indicates, changes in the designs were made once work commenced.

The juxtaposition of real urns with an antique vase seemingly overflowing with foliage is, of course, intentional. The furnishings and their placement have been deliberately chosen for their visual effect.

Despite its elegance and striking profile, Trump Tower in Manhattan is not very much unlike most modern apartment complexes—dull and bare bones in composition. For anyone desiring something more than a dramatic view of the city from a *pied-à-terre* in the sky, Hellmut and Hellgah Dieken have provided a provocative alternative. With flair and brilliance, the artists have transformed a sterile box into a highly imaginative setting.

The pedestrian entryway to a Bel Air apartment was strikingly transformed with painted decoration. The artful juxtaposition of architectural design elements such as the balustrade and the ceiling cornice with background floral motifs is a particular feature of the Diekens' work. This "layering" of painted designs both heightens the illusion of space and cunningly distorts perspective just enough to allow the viewer to know that the whole composition is purely imaginative.

An entry hall in the Palais Ritter in Austria is representative of the traditional work completed by the Diekens in Europe over the past twenty years. The wall panel and ceiling dome designs are painted in oil on canvas and incorporate various trompe l'oeil elements. Soft blues and greens are combined with beige and tans to create a light, airy effect throughout the rather imposing space.

A portion of a thirty-foot Caribbean landscape mural, illustrated here, includes touches of trompe l'oeil. Hellmut and Hellgah Dieken, shown below at work on another section of the mural, usually paint on canvas but also make use of chrome, glass, wood, plastic, and plaster. They have so perfected their paint formula that a mural such as this can be cleaned even with soap and water without losing any of its finish or detail.

Combining Architecture and Ornament

Caryl Hall remembers well the day she first discovered the work of Philip Jordan. Driving down the familiar streets of Huntington, Long Island, she came across the Canterbury Ales Restaurant. The building looked completely different. In fact, windows now appeared in a wall that had been largely blank only a few weeks earlier. Being well versed in the technique of trompe l'oeil mural painting, Hall realized quickly that someone had artfully transformed the façade with layers of paint. Curious as to who had done the work, she inquired and was told that the author was a young man by the name of Philip Jordan. Where might he be? Hall was told that he had recently left to paint in France. She admits that she was both disappointed and relieved. Disappointed because meeting anyone with a similar background and talent as hers would be an interesting

Opposite page: **From 1979 to 1983 Philip Jordan was active in a Paris-based league of architects, artists, designers, poets, and writers from many countries. Poetic License was the name the group took, and architectural painting, led by Jordan, was one of the activities they pursued. Paris is blessed with an abundance of architectural decoration, but the sanc-** **tuary along the rue du Faubourg St. Honoré, occupied by the American ambassador, lacked panache. One wall of the inner courtyard, in fact, was an almost total boring blank. Jordan and his unusual team of assistants filled this void with windows reflecting sky and clouds, decorative pilasters, moldings, keystones, and capitals.** **For the nearby U. S. Consulate, Jordan designed and executed the entry hall, *below*, where guards check in visitors. The space had all the charm of a state motor vehicles' office, he explains, and demanded a witty, cheerful treatment. The trompe l'oeil panels, painted on canvas, and *faux* marble floor greatly improved the vestibule.**

experience; relieved because his absence from the scene meant that there was one less architectural painter with whom to compete. That was in 1982. Today Hall and Jordan work together, having joined artistic forces in 1983 upon his return from France. His love is of rendering architectural detail; hers, the painting of landscape scenes and picturesque motifs. Both are Long Island natives and move easily in the interior design circles emanating from New York City and Florida. Their commissions are both residential and commercial and include all forms of applied art, even the decoration of furniture. They bring to Caryl Hall Studios of Cold Spring Harbor a combined total of forty-three years of experience, a record matched by few American decorative painters.

Poetic License

A close-up view of a keystone and capital painted on the façade of the U.S. Ambassador's residence in Paris illustrates how a skillful trompe l'oeil painter can simulate architectural decoration. Jordan, trained at the Kansas City Art Institute, precisely matched details from other parts of the building's façade, creating the illusion of depth through shadow and tone. Equally skilled is the imitation of the roughly shaped and coursed stonework.

Jordan, poised with an assistant on the scaffolding of the Canterbury Ales Restaurant building in Huntington, Long Island, worked on this project for over three months. As can be seen from the "before" picture, the wall to be decorated was an ugly expanse of plaster over brick. The artist used the surface like a giant canvas, adding six windows to the two already present. One of the new windows is always "open," regardless of the weather. Other *faux* openings have shades which are drawn to the same level.

How well Jordan matched the main facade is illustrated in the photograph at the bottom. The new side wall needs only a *faux* air conditioner to complete the illusion.

Philip Jordan and Caryl Hall worked together with a team of assistants on the decoration of a master bedroom, *opposite page*, in a North Shore, Long Island, home. The generous 30' by 40' space allowed them to divide the room into sleeping and daytime areas, each with distinctive decorative elements. The *faux* marble floor, which seemingly flows right into the trompe l'oeil murals at each side of the bed, unites the real and illusionary spaces. Jordan designed and executed the architectural motifs; Hall, the flora and fauna and landscape scenes.

The full range of the decorative finishes and techniques mastered by Jordan and Hall is illustrated in two views of a hallway recently painted in a Long Island home. The walls of the front hall have been marbleized and softly glazed; a trompe l'oeil niche is the background for a floral panel. A few leaves from this overflowing urn are casually incorporated in the *faux* mosaic stone floor.

The rear hall, rather than ending abruptly in a blank wall, appears to open up to a parterre garden. A floor in imitation of cobblestone continues in unbroken perspective beyond the actual space. *Faux* wood trelliswork is used to decorate the walls; trailing flora appears to wind its way in and out of the hallway.

The Ceiling Lady

Because of her interest in restoring stenciled ceilings to their former glory, Judith Hendershot is known by preservation experts everywhere as "the ceiling lady." Any woman daring enough to climb ladders and scaffolding and to work for long hours with her head held back at an unnatural angle deserves such a sobriquet.

Nevertheless, it is the quality of her work in re-creating the designs of past masters as well as in executing original new patterns that has gained her recognition. Like many other American decorative painters drawn to the revival of ornamentalism in the 1970s, Hendershot is largely self-taught. For some time her "studio" was nothing more than a makeshift kitchen table-drawing board in her suburban Evanston, Illinois, home. From there—armed with sketches, templates, and paints—she would set forth to decorate ceilings, walls, and floors in many homes throughout the Chicago area. The first commissions were small but important in that they provided training on the job. Hendershot's office is still in her home, but her portfolio has been greatly enlarged. Her first important commission was the restoration of Louis Sullivan's stencil decoration for the boxes in Chicago's world-famous Auditorium Theatre in 1978. Since then she has executed previously unknown designs by Daniel Burnham, another Chicago architectural master; translated the work of the English Victorian artist Christopher Dresser; and re-created the designs of a gifted Arts and Crafts painter of the early 1900s.

The lobby of Chicago's Railway Exchange Building, now known as Sante Fe Center, is today more handsome and complete in ornamentation than when it was built in 1904. Architect Daniel Burnham, author of the famous Chicago Plan of 1909 and builder of the 1893 World's Columbian Exposition, intended that the steel skylight beams be decorated with a stencil design of his choosing. The work, however, was not undertaken until recently by Judith Hendershot and her assistants. With patient fidelity, they followed Burnham's design, the original of which is shown here.

Hendershot drew up a new master stencil based on the Burnham pattern for the Railway Exchange. The design is slightly more open and regular than the original, two factors which made it somewhat easier to render. As originally intended, the design was worked in two basic colors—gold and terra cotta.

Almost all elements of the two-story lobby were restored. Crystalline translucent glass was used to glaze the skylight, and a patterned marble floor, specified by Burnham but never installed, was laid.

Moving their templates from place to place, Judith Hendershot and two assistants completed the work of decorating the ceiling in two weeks' time. Their old-fashioned work often drew the interest of other members of the building restoration crew who could view it from the top of the skylight.

The building now serves as the headquarters of the Santa Fe Southern Pacific Corp. In 1982 it was officially listed on the National Register of Historic Places.

Built in the early 1900s, the Murray Theatre at Ravinia Park, on Chicago's North Shore, is the home of the Ravinia Music Festival. Approximately 500 feet of the wood ceiling in the Arts and Crafts-style concert hall had to be replaced in 1983. Hendershot and assistants restenciled the original 14" border in sections varying in size from 4" to several feet. As can be seen, the pattern is very complicated, involving many twists and turns and an imaginative palette of four subtle colors. Stenciling across such narrow boards as these was a particularly difficult assignment.

A modern office space such as an elevator lobby and reception area need not be undistinguished. The Chicago investment counseling firm of Stein Roe and Farnham turned to Hendershot for inspiration. Two complementary stencil designs employing twelve colors were chosen to decorate the beams and to comprise a frieze. The patterns were stenciled on canvas, which was then applied to the plaster surfaces.

Hendershot has decorated many Chicago-area homes and recently completed work on the cathedral ceiling of a Lake Forest Tudor Revival residence. Sixteen border panels outline the rustic beams and give the handsome ceiling as much interest as the elaborately furnished living room itself.

This type of decoration might be as effectively applied to the vaulted ceilings popular today in many contemporary homes. The ornamentation reflects the artist's belief that "stenciling can be used wherever people want to beautify their surroundings with personalized, unique, custom decoration." Judith Hendershot often draws her designs from classic nineteenth-century sources. In the case of the Lake Forest home, she adapted a traditional pattern in color and line to suit the furnishings and to complement the architectural detail of the room.

Order Out of Chaos

The first visit to EverGreene Painting Studios is something of a shock. After dodging the debris and pushcarts of Manhattan's West 36th Street, one finally arrives in front of number 365, a typical rundown veteran of urban architectural warfare. Dimly visible in the windows is an assortment of dusty bags of Italian glazing compound, several marbleized panels, and a scattering of small architectural elements. Upon prying the door open so as not to disturb its shakey hinges and stepping forth into a sea of rolled and unfurled canvases, the only thought, a question, is: Can this be the famed EverGreene Studios, the place where the most elegant, the most fashionable of decorative artifacts are dreamed up and executed? From a precariously perched gallery at one end of the long room comes reassurance from a secretary trying to field a telephone call over a roar of contending voices. "Yes, Jeff is here today and, no, he can't talk to you. . . ." Jeff is Jeff Greene, creator and director of this unique enterprise, the studios' business manager and salesman, an accomplished artist and designer. Indelibly preppy and infectiously en-

thusiastic, he might still be a student at the Art Institute of Chicago. So enthralled is he with his profession and that of his colleagues, that the visitor is instantly put at ease. It seems perfectly natural to be invited to share one corner of a desk at which Jeff and three others are at work in the minuscule garret. Drawings for the ceiling of the Vice-President's office in Washington are pinned to the walls, designs for a construction fence on Madison Avenue spill out of a corner shelf. Everything seems to be in complete disorder, but Jeff makes sense of it all.

"Everyone I have working for me is an artist in his own right," he explains. "Each person develops his own area of expertise—drafting, color, glazing, marbling. I have to act as a kind of conductor who understands the properties of all the various instruments and knows how to combine them to get the right effect." There are usually a dozen to fifteen such artists working at any given time for EverGreene in New York and various locations throughout the East Coast and Midwest. The firm, in existence only since 1980, has carried out the designs of such recognized artists as Richard Haas and Peter

It is rare for so many members of the EverGreene troupe to be in New York at the same time. Among the group are always current and former art students who have drifted into the world of architectural painting from more formal disciplines. Children of the staff are also attracted to the bustling scene. Owner and founder Jeff Greene is standing in the last row, center, sporting a gray tweed jacket.

Decoration of the lobby of New York's midtown Crown Building (*opposite page*) was completed in the summer of 1984. Peter Saari was the designer of the stenciled trompe l'oeil coffered ceiling. EverGreene's crew worked with artist Lynn Goodpasture, whose work is illustrated on pages 160-69.

The decoration of the Crown Building in New York involved several months' work. The vaulted space is not unlike that of a cathedral, and its design assumed Renaissance dimensions. A decorative keystone rendered in trompe l'oeil caps the towering front portico, and around this are bands of *faux* plasterwork. Decorative panels and vignettes of classical Italian scenes form a frieze below the illusionary coffered ceiling.

Marino. At the same time, Greene and his colleagues are the authors of most of the projects they execute for commercial, residential, and public clients. They have achieved an enviable reputation for their dramatic and whimsical trompe l'oeil murals and painstakingly correct historic restoration work. Success in achieving such artistic logic and order only makes the frenzied disarray of EverGreene's office all the more awesome.

Construction fences are not what they used to be, at least not in sophisticated urban settings. EverGreene has specialized in murals which serve both utilitarian and commercial purposes: such a fence protects the building site from intruders while at the same time attracting the attention of the business community and would-be tenants.

A highly imaginative Art Deco construction fence for the Museum Tower office building site in Miami was designed by Richard Haas and executed by EverGreene in the spring of 1985. The wall extends well over 100 linear feet, and construction and decoration required a crew of from six to eight members. The work is entirely trompe l'oeil.

Executing designs by Richard Haas is never a simple matter. The complexity of the Art Deco decoration is readily visible in the panel illustrated at the left. Haas himself admits the difficulty of interpreting such a design and expresses his pleasure that there has been "a marked improvement in the quality level since Greene has done my large projects."

The construction fence shows how effectively mural painting can be used to suggest architectural dimension. This is especially evident in the forms chosen for the false front constructed around the site of the Parc Vendôme apartment building restoration on West 57th Street in Manhattan. Madeleine Speer was the designer of the project embracing windows, walls, columns, and fencing rendered in trompe l'oeil.

The Limited, a retail clothing store new to New York, advertised its coming to the city in a high-style manner befitting the company's merchandising image. The architectural firm of Beyer Binder Bell designed a construction fence which cleverly echoed the lines of the former Louis Sherry store at 62nd Street and Madison (seen in black and white at left). The complicated superstructure was constructed by the building crew and painted by EverGreene in the fall of 1984. The work included precise rendering of the early building's ornamental entrances.

Cappreccio's Restaurant (below) in Atlanta was a handsome building before the façade was painted by EverGreene in 1985, but bland in color and composition. All that was changed by accenting the facade's architectural detailing and adding trompe l'oeil elements such as window moldings and a false entrance at one side of the building.

Life-size painted figures and a trompe l'oeil façade created a neighborly image for the Borough Park construction site in Brooklyn. EverGreene designed and executed the project in the spring of 1983.

Well-wrought *faux* finishes have a beauty and integrity of their very own. Marble, one of the most costly building materials, lends itself to painted imitation because of its endless variations in pattern, its lustre, and its luminescence. Designer Richard Haas took advantage of these qualities in his plan for the floor, walls, and ceiling of the lobby of the Chestnut Place apartment building in Chicago. EverGreene executed the intricate mosaic design of all surfaces, including the center column. Haas's design was based on the decoration of the church of San Miniato al Monte in Florence, Italy.

Jeff Greene designed the gigantic trompe l'oeil curtain on canvas which enclosed the construction site of Metropolitan Square in Washington, D.C. The inviting promise of a soon-to-be-realized public space, replete with painted people, is partially and cleverly unveiled in one corner of the Garfinckel's department store façade. Greene especially enjoys such wacky and witty visual tricks.

Until he founded his studio in 1980, Jeff Greene made a living from house painting. While he remains devoted to his first real love, mural painting, residential decoration involving a variety of painted techniques and finishes continues to intrigue him and his associates. A New York apartment, designed by architect Peter Marino and Ira Schachner, presented Ever-Greene's team of painters with many opportunities to display their talents.

The living room features antique wood cabinetry and heavy furnishings. A simple wood floor has been transformed into what appears to be inlaid wood flooring. The various paint finishes complement the fine woods and inlays of the room's cabinets. The walls and ceiling are painted white, the dentil cornice being defined by gold striping. The elegance of the interior is further enhanced by the addition of a stenciled gold ceiling border. Artist Lynn Goodpasture, a frequent contributor to EverGreene projects, assisted with the stenciling.

The Guerlain Department in New York's Bergdorf Goodman store is one of the city's most luxurious commercial spaces. The design of the salon called for EverGreene to marbleize, glaze, and stencil the walls, ceiling, and furnishings. Soft, warm colors are used throughout the semicircular space to endow it with a feeling of ease and elegance. The dome is stencil-painted in slightly lighter colors than the walls and counters to create the illusion of greater height. All surfaces are glazed to give them the look of graceful age. These painted effects could have been created using real materials at much greater cost. True marble, however, would probably lack the warmth and edge of the painter's artifice which is so appealing in a high-style cosmetics salon.

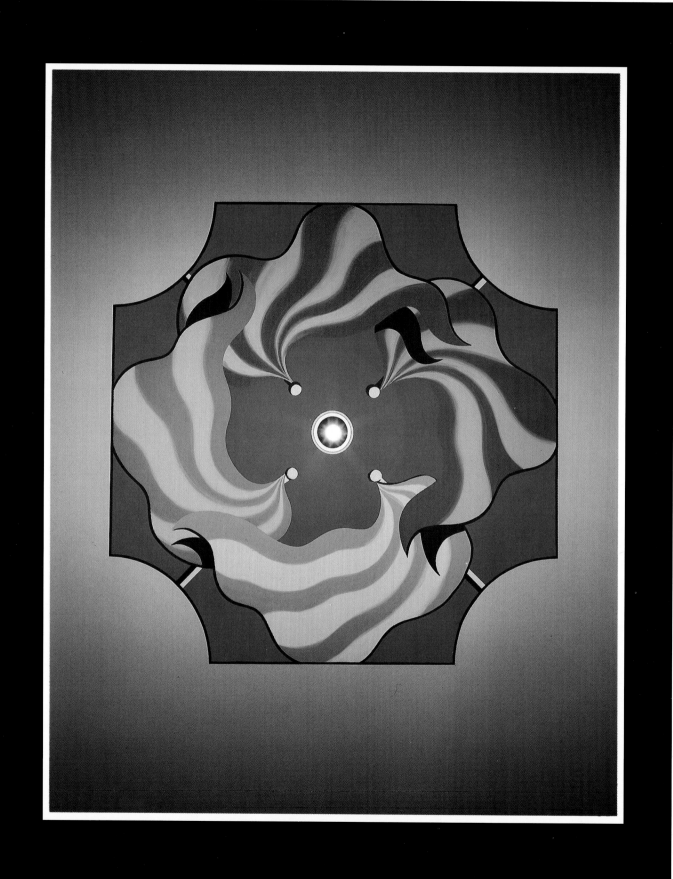

Beyond Tradition

The name Megan Parry is practically synonymous with the revival of the art of stenciling in America. Even before the publication of her illustrated instructional book, *Stenciling*, in 1977, she was the object of a broad following. She inspired countless imitators who found the seemingly simple stenciling technique of decoration an easy way to add traditional motifs to barren spaces, however inappropriate or badly rendered the designs might be. As another stenciling specialist has explained, "If you had only one bird, but wanted a flock; if you had a single tree, but wanted a forest, then stenciling would be the art form to use." The same images repeated ad nauseam, however, in interior after interior, quickly lose their appeal and value. This is a point not lost on Megan Parry, whose art has grown with every season since she first began stenciling in 1972. Although thoroughly familiar with the work of past generations, including the early American itinerant artists and the late-Victorian decorators of England and America, she is continually exploring new forms and motifs. Educated at Bennington College and the University of Colorado, she has worked out of her Boulder, Colorado, studio on an exceptionally diverse selection of commissions, including ceilings and walls of public buildings, banks, restaurants, office complexes, and private homes. In the process, Parry has developed her talent for freehand painting and *faux* finishes. Stenciled motifs are still very much a part of her repertoire, but if she were to write a new instructional book, it would have to be entitled *Stenciling and Beyond*.

Painted ceilings incorporating freehand and stenciled elements have become an important part of Megan Parry's work. "There is no painless way to stencil on the ceiling," she has written, and hand-painted ornamentation is an even more difficult and exciting challenge to her.

The 10-foot square ceiling entitled "Palio," and shown on the opposite page, is almost entirely hand-painted. Illustrated below is one of Parry's most inventive ceiling designs, completed in 1984 for the social hall of the Colorado School for the Deaf and Blind in Colorado Springs.

The illusionary effects of trompe l'oeil decoration intrigue Parry, and she is expert at capturing them. The design chosen for the ceiling and cove of the Old Main Chapel Theatre at the University of Colorado is a joyful pastiche of traditional eighteenth-century forms. The center sky is surrounded by trompe l'oeil cupids and fanciful moldings containing ornamental flourishes. Not visible in these photographs are a *faux* marble proscenium arch and columns.

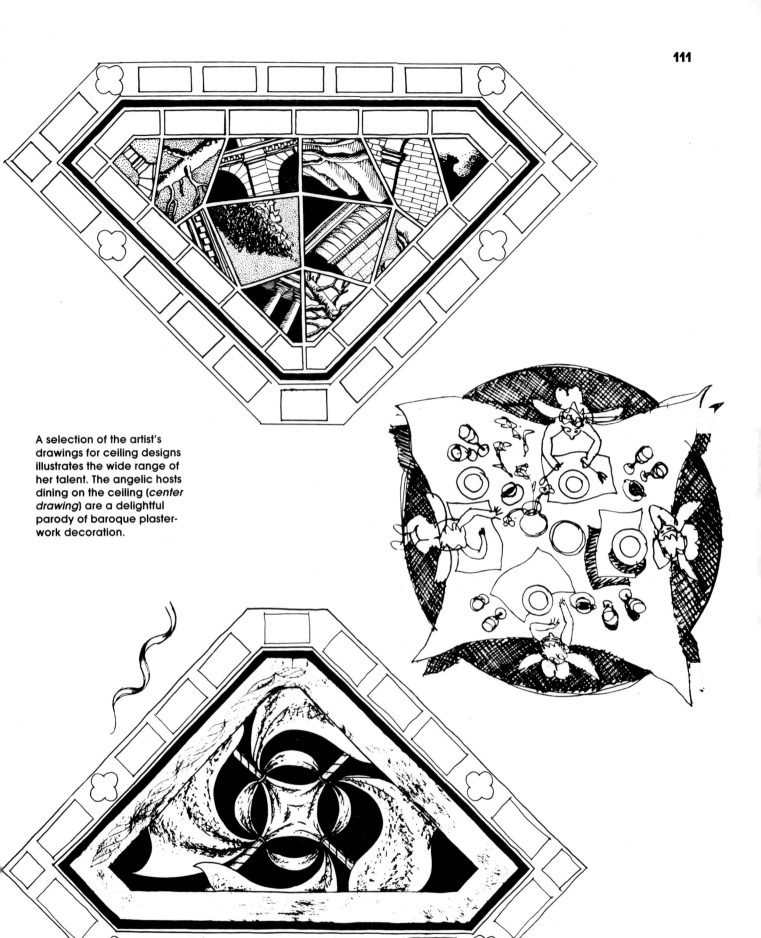

A selection of the artist's drawings for ceiling designs illustrates the wide range of her talent. The angelic hosts dining on the ceiling (*center drawing*) are a delightful parody of baroque plaster-work decoration.

Mural painting is now an important part of Parry's work. In the two scenes illustrated on this page and opposite, she has combined stenciled and freehand painting. The painted telephone niche, entitled "L'Etat C'est Moi," is a wild composition which brings together stylized columns, capitals, abstract motifs, human figures, and traditional stencil designs. The drinking fountain niche design is similarly complex and makes playful use of trompe l'oeil effects. The rendering of such ordinary public spaces in a highly imaginative, almost surreal, manner is a far cry from the work of the ordinary architectural painter.

A running stencil pattern is the perfect motif for a bannister. Note, however, that Parry has purposefully angled the design off-center. She has created more than a decorative effect. The bannister has become a work of art in itself, something to be studied and not simply used.

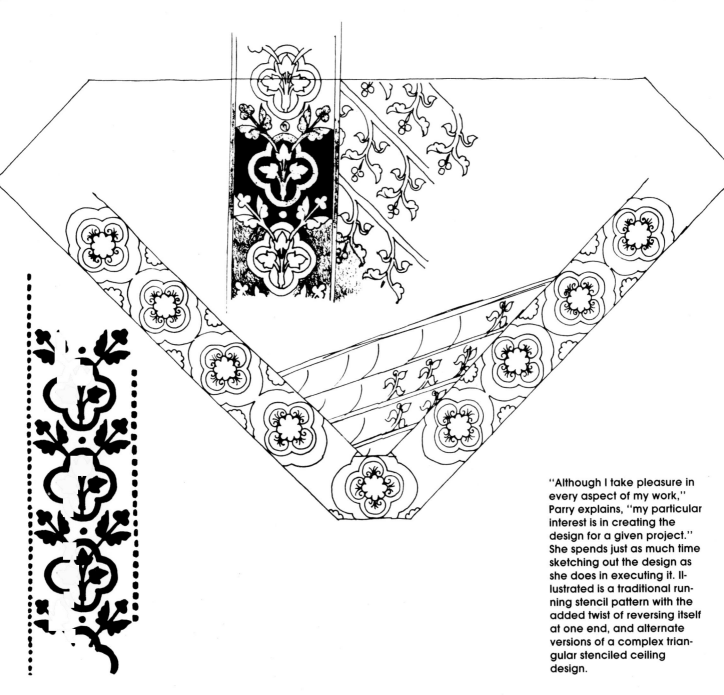

"Although I take pleasure in every aspect of my work," Parry explains, "my particular interest is in creating the design for a given project." She spends just as much time sketching out the design as she does in executing it. Illustrated is a traditional running stencil pattern with the added twist of reversing itself at one end, and alternate versions of a complex triangular stenciled ceiling design.

British Tradition in America

American decorating and design firms such as The Rambusch Co. of New York, the Edward K. Perry Co. of Boston, and A.F. Heinsbergen of Los Angeles have played an important role in maintaining high standards

of American craftsmanship since the late nineteenth century. During the many years since the 1930s when anything ornamental in architecture and interior design was derided as hopelessly dated by the trend-setters,

The rotunda walls and dome of the Pennsylvania State Capitol were cleaned and restored from top to bottom. The restoration called for two coats of oil paint, gold leaf, and the application of Dutch metal. Forty samples of paint were taken, analyzed, documented, and catalogued before the work was begun.

these distinguished companies of artisans managed to stay alive. Now they are in the enviable position of being able to choose their commissions from a large pool of public and private clients. With the formal arrival of the venerable British design firm of Campbell Smith & Company on these shores in 1982, the importance of the American preservation scene has been acknowledged. Campbell Smith, whose work can be seen in every stateroom of Buckingham Palace, at Westminster Abbey, and St. Paul's Cathedral, personifies the English decorative tradition, a heritage shared with North America. The transplanting of the London-based firm was easily accomplished because of this common link. Campbell Smith entered into partnership with The Biltmore Company of Asheville, North Carolina, to form Biltmore, Campbell, Smith Restorations. Biltmore, the baronial Vanderbilt family complex, a citadel of Anglo-Saxon sensibility in the western North Carolina mountains, has attracted the talent of countless craftsmen since it was first established in the 1890s. In the 1970s, the house and garden were extensively restored by the estate's own artists and technicians. Their work superbly prepared them for undertaking commissions elsewhere as Biltmore, Campbell, Smith.

Almost all of the firm's principals are American, including William A.V. Cecil, president; Susanne Brendel-Pandich, projects manager; Richard N. King, operations manager; and Barney D. Lamar, conservator. Trained on both sides of the Atlantic, they move easily from one complex project to another, undertaking everything from the design and restoration of all forms of painted decoration to the cleaning and restoration of mural and easel paintings. Already among their credits are San Francisco Plantation near New Orleans, the ballroom of the Atlanta-Biltmore Hotel, and the grand parlor of Flagler College in Saint Augustine, Florida. Nearing completion, after two years' work, is the restoration of the murals and rotunda of the Pennsylvania State Capitol in Harrisburg. Now underway is the restoration of the floor in the Vice-President's office, Washington, D.C., and the Old Library of the Tennessee State Capitol in Nashville.

118

St. Augustine's Flagler College is located in the former Ponce de Leon Hotel, a splendid survivor of nineteenth-century Florida tourism. Henry Flagler, a railroad magnate, commissioned the firm of Carrère and Hastings to design the resort complex in the late 1880s. The interior of the three-and-a-half story building is distinguished by murals, Tiffany glass, mosaics, plaster ornamentation, and painted ceilings.

Biltmore, Campbell, Smith restored the grand parlor and adjoining space in 1984. The work included the repainting and reglazing of the plasterwork forming the ornate chimney piece and the repainting and replastering of the ceiling. Extensive overpainting had to be removed from the ceiling before restoration work could begin. This was especially important in the painted ceiling panels of the area adjacent to the main hall. A detail of the elaborate design by Virgilio Tojetti for these panels is shown at the right.

Before work could commence at the Pennsylvania State Capitol, intricate scaffolding had to be erected. Universal Builders of New York, a firm responsible for the Statue of Liberty's reconstruction superstructure, erected the maze of pipes and plywood decking. Rolling towers were used to reach the upper levels of the dome.

The palatial State Capitol, dedicated in 1906 and designed in the Italian Renaissance style by Joseph M. Huston, has a dome which reaches a height of 272 feet. Edwin Austin Abbey, a Philadelphia-born painter who gained renown in England and the United States for his historical illustrations and murals, was chosen in 1902 to execute massive murals within the arches of the rotunda. It is these four paintings which required the special expertise of the Biltmore, Campbell, Smith team.

Each of the murals spans 38 feet in length and 22 feet in height to the center of the arch. Over the years each has suffered considerable water damage and has been subjected to hasty overpainting. Illustrated is the west mural, "Science Revealing Treasures of the Earth," a theme especially relevant to the economic history of the Commonwealth. Before this mural could be restored and treated for future conservation, special studies were made of the moisture content, the damage of salt deposits, and the chemical make-up of paints and finishes. The extent of the moisture damage is represented on the drawing.

MOISTURE MEASUREMENTS

① SURFACE READING 40
② " " 62   ⑥ SURFACE READING 5
③ " " MAX   ⑦ " " 80
④ " " MAX   ⑧ " " 5
⑤ DEPTH 1" MAX   Ⓐ Ⓑ Salt Samples

Proper restoration and conservation of the murals required that they be removed from the plaster walls and laid flat. Edwin Abbey had painted them on canvas which could be removed—with exceptional care. How to remove the murals efficiently and effectively with each of them already in the damaged condition apparent here in "The Spirit of Vulcan," was the most interesting challenge faced by the Biltmore, Campbell, Smith crew. Their solution is an ingenious one: a mechanism of cylinders on a track around which the canvas could be wound and then lowered to the plywood platform for restoration. Workers standing on an adjustable platform used spatulas to free the canvas from the plaster wall.

Among the first steps to be accomplished after the canvas had been removed was to clean away old varnish and overpainting. The back of each mural was also cleaned of plaster and white lead adhesive and any later canvas additions. Layers of mulberry tissue and a synthetic substance were then applied to strengthen and consolidate the canvas.

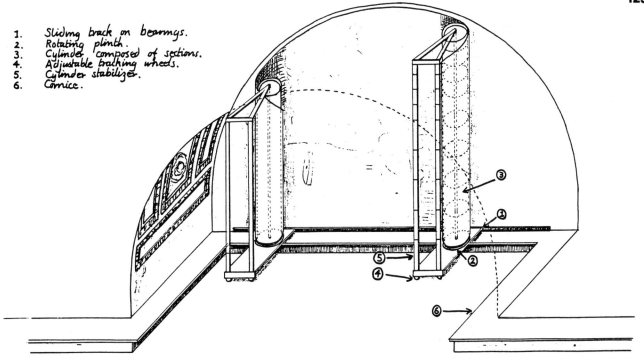

1. Sliding track on bearings.
2. Rotating plinth.
3. Cylinder composed of sections.
4. Adjustable tracking wheels.
5. Cylinder stabilizer.
6. Cornice.

An important reason for removing the murals from the walls was to allow them to be remounted on solid support structures held away from the walls. The paintings would then not be as subject to future moisture or structural problems. The framing system would also make it easier to remove the murals when they did require maintenance.

The intricate scaffolding superstructure allowed for work to take place on various aspects of the project at the same time. The restoration team estimated that this overall device saved them several years of work.

126

San Francisco Plantation, an hour upriver from New Orleans, was extensively restored in the mid-1970s. Restoration of painted decoration throughout the 1853-56 mansion required cleaning, the removal of overpainting, and meticulous duplication of the original designs. San Francisco, administered by a private foundation, is now open to the public. Henry A. Dornsife and Sons served as the interior designer of the restoration, and Koch and Wilson as the architects.

The Atlanta Biltmore, a grand hotel in the Georgian Revival style, is now an Atlanta landmark. Built in 1924 and designed by Leonard Shultze, also the architect of the more famous Los Angeles Biltmore, the building suffered many aesthetic indignities until preservationists came to the rescue. The traditional elegance of the hotel is captured in this in-progress photograph of a portion of one of two ballrooms restored by Biltmore, Campbell, Smith in 1985. The plastered and painted cornice and ceiling now have depth and imaginative composition; the repainted neoclassical motifs possess a new charm.

Portable Illusion

Imagine being able to move an opening in a wall from one side of a room to another. If the niche is only a painted canvas, a likeness having the depth and definition of a three-dimensional object, the subject can be hung almost anywhere it creates interest. Such a magical transformation of space is a stock in trade for Tish and John Albright, trompe l'oeil artists whose work is known throughout the United States. From their suburban Philadelphia studio they produce artwork for hotels, restaurants, department stores, private homes, airports, corporations, and museums. They are mural painters first and foremost, knowledgeable in the techniques and finishes of architectural painting, but uninvolved in the many restoration projects that occupy the time of most architectural painters. Since their graduation from the Philadelphia Museum School of Art in the 1960s, the Albrights have been fascinated by the transformation of space through trompe l'oeil techniques—a closet door that is made to look like a well-stocked bookcase, a would-be marble colonnade, a fireplace that couldn't possibly work, a make-believe landscape of the ancient world so real that people attempt to walk into it. Much of Tish and John Albright's work is performed jointly, but John specializes in small trompe l'oeil canvases of particular charm and ingenuity that might be called architectural still-lifes. Inspired by an old doorway or an ornamental column seen on the streets of Philadelphia, he will render the subject on canvas, adding perhaps a composition of apples or pears, a surprising but artful addition. Whimsical paintings of this type can be moved from place to place wherever fancy dictates.

One of John Albright's trompe l'oeil still-lifes is shown opposite. The brickwork is expertly rendered in all of its textural qualities, but the air of verisimilitude is created with shadowing and tone. The juxtaposition of the sliced eggplant and its draping further accentuate the three dimensionality of the painting.

Tish and John Albright are pictured here in one of their rare free moments. They founded their own painting studio in 1970 and have since produced murals for clients in the United States, Europe, the Middle East, Central and South America, and Canada.

A modern Stonehenge is suggested by the massing of geometric shapes represented in a painting which seems to extend beyond its frame. Projected against the sky, with light and shadow adding dimension, the slabs have a fantasy appearance suggesting a journey beyond time.

The source of John Albright's inspiration for the painting below was a decorative stone panel and rondel in an entryway column. The stonework has been faithfully replicated, down to the pitted and cracked surface. As in his other small still-lifes, Albright has used an architectural element as the setting for a formal, draped composition. The study might very well have been taken from the canvas of a seventeenth-century Flemish still-life painter.

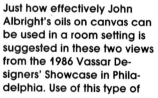

Just how effectively John Albright's oils on canvas can be used in a room setting is suggested in these two views from the 1986 Vassar Designers' Showcase in Philadelphia. Use of this type of artwork over a mantel rather than a mirror or landscape is a welcome change. Equally interesting is the fake fireplace screen of glass on which birch logs have been painted.

John Albright is adept at rendering stonework of various types, including marble and granite. Panels such as these are increasingly popular in postmodern residential interiors. They enlarge nonexistent space and endow it with visual interest. An art critic has written admiringly that Tish and John Albright "make a living by making other people look twice." These paintings are worth much more than a double take.

From Art Deco to Postmodern

Artist David Cohn anticipates fads and fancies. Long before Art Deco was embraced by the fashionable, he was intrigued by the style's curving lines; when linoleum patterns from the 1920s were being consigned to the dustbin, Cohn was saving scraps and old catalogs of designs, so taken was he with their muted colors and complex patterns. Five years ago linoleum was no longer in production in America; today, "antique" designs are being reproduced. It is not difficult for Cohn to be ahead of the times because he is a true student of the fine and decorative arts, trained at the Pratt Institute of Design in the 1960s and still as enthusiastic about discovering new sources of design as he was in his twenties. Working from his apartment-studio in New York's Greenwich Village, he is at the center of a constant cultural revolution, an atmosphere in which yesterday's trash is more than likely to be revived as today's treasure. Like his former partner David Fisch, friend Nancy Kintisch, and first employer Caryl Hall, he was born in the New York area and discovered mural painting by chance. Like them also, little of his work is in restoration, but consists of commissions for contemporary work. He prefers residential projects on a large scale involving painted floors or walls. "Everyone in New York wants glazing and marbleizing done these days," he explains, but such technical exercises leave him somewhat bored if they are an end in themselves. Give him a blank wall to paint, however, and he will dramatically transform it.

David Cohn used stencils and graining combs to imitate a pattern (*opposite page*) found in an old woven fabric. Because of its narrow boards, the plain wooden floor of the New York apartment was difficult to paint, but the results more than justified the extra effort. As shown below, the painted surface serves as a handsome base for the neutral colored, streamlined furnishings of the room.

The earthenware paving of a chapel in the cathedral of Siena, Italy (*left*), provided the inspiration for another New York apartment floor design. Photographed on a trip to Italy, the tile pattern obsessed Cohn until he could find a client who would agree to its reproduction. Even the wear and tear of the centuries is imitated. The original gold and light and dark blue colors were also reproduced.

A lighter and more elegant pattern was chosen by Cohn to crisscross the fine wood floors of a New York apartment dining room. Garlands of morning glories are entwined with butterflies and other leafy motifs. The client's fine collection of decorative porcelains, displayed on the Welsh sideboard, prompted Cohn's choice of design. Given two protective coats of varnish, the floor decoration should survive as long as the china does. In common with most other architectural painters, Cohn avoids the artificial high finish of polyurethane.

Opposite page: The Art Deco design of this New York living room floor is one of David Cohn's masterpieces. The apartment owner prides himself on his collection of 1930s theater lobby furniture, of which the sofa is a classic example. The floor design is not a reproduction, but an interpretation of an ideal Deco design. Cohn has stenciled all of it against a black field, one area carrying a wavy, overlapping pattern that appears to be fraying at the edges; several of the elements have broken loose. The other end of the room is outlined in an amusing border made up of high-style artifacts of a cocktail party —shaker, ashtray, glass, swizzle sticks, and champagne bottle. Even the cigarette smoke is captured.

Bathrooms, notoriously conventional in their appointments and decoration, are always a challenge to an architectural painter. In an apartment building, this room is often a claustrophobic space without natural light. David Cohn transformed the room by giving it the appearance of a tent interior, its sides drawn back to reveal beach and ocean views. Elements of the overhead floral design are repeated in the painted ceiling and side drapes.

Cohn's painting is straightforward in this instance, avoiding the visual tricks of trompe l'oeil perspective. The irregularity of the wall surfaces would have made shadowing difficult to achieve, but various elements of the design, as in the beach scene, wrap around the angles and contribute to an illusion of depth.

An old silk-screened wallpaper in rich, vibrant colors is the basis for a large scenic mural. Cohn has painted layer over layer of color, incorporating such elements as trelliswork and various forms of animal life, such as a lizard. Large-scale interior mural projects are David Cohn's favorite commissions and will sometimes occupy him for months at a time.

Respectful Restoration

Scotland's loss is America's decided gain. John Canning still retains the soft burr of a native Glaswegian, but in the seventeen years that he has worked in the United States he has acquired the businesslike de-

Karen Bussolini

The Senate Chamber of the Connecticut State Capitol was the first large space to be restored in the building. Formerly the Library, it was converted in 1910 with the addition of galleries. Canning and associates in the Capitol Architect's office spent months studying the space, taking color samples and making tracings of surviving stencil patterns once they were unearthed. The square brown and gold designs, seen in the lower left of the photograph, were found behind a gallery side wall. In the 1910 conversion they had been completely hidden from sight.

meanor of a successful American entrepreneur. Canning does not chat about his work but, rather, in a rush to get back to it, expounds on the immense amount of time required for careful restoration. Keeping up with him as he strides through the Connecticut State Capitol complex in Hartford, explaining his present major project as he goes, requires a special effort on the part of the visitor. But, then, nearly everything that John Canning undertakes in the field of historic preservation becomes a cause. The list of projects is impressive—the restoration of the ceiling and wall decoration of Yale's Battell Chapel; Charter Oak Temple, the oldest synagogue in Connecticut; and now the Senate Chamber, Hall of Flags, and atriums of the landmark 1872-1880 capitol.

For a man who began a five-year apprenticeship to a Glasgow painting and decorating firm at the age of fifteen and studied church decoration, there is much to be proud of. He has two apprentices of his own and a firm, John Canning Painting & Decorating, which often has two or three projects proceeding simultaneously. It gives him special pleasure that he is now devoting considerable time to the restoration of the work of a fellow Scotsman, William McPherson, who was chosen in 1877 to execute the interior decoration of the high-Victorian Gothic capitol designed by Richard Michell Upjohn. Uncovering and restoring McPherson's extraordinary designs has been as much a labor of love as a serious business proposition.

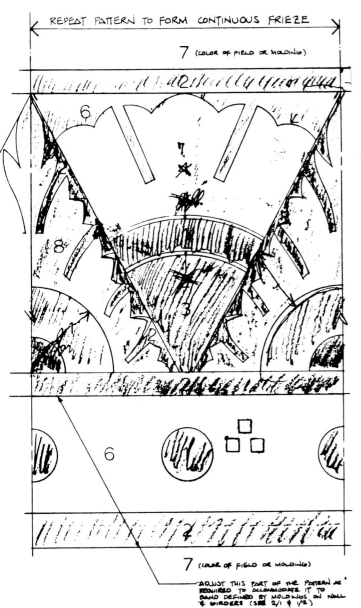

Upjohn's State Capitol was completed in 1880, a year after this engraving was made. The architect would have prefered a clock tower rather than a dome, but the Board of Capitol Commissioners upheld their preference for the latter form in 1873.

All the re-created stencil patterns are a composite of William McPherson's original designs and colors. The frieze pattern shown here in a working drawing is found in the left center of the color photograph on the opposite page.

After the wall surfaces of the Senate Chamber had been cleaned and repaired, the re-stenciling could begin. The general division of the squares was lined out and the outlines of the alternating patterns were stenciled using templates of stable acrylic. Colors were then added to the patterns. Left for last was the delineation and painting of the rosette centers.

The walls were then ready for further stenciling and striping. The frieze pattern appearing below the decorative plasterwork is the same used above the square rosettes (*see* p. 142). A rich reddish shade and peacock blue were applied to wall areas without stencil decoration or striping.

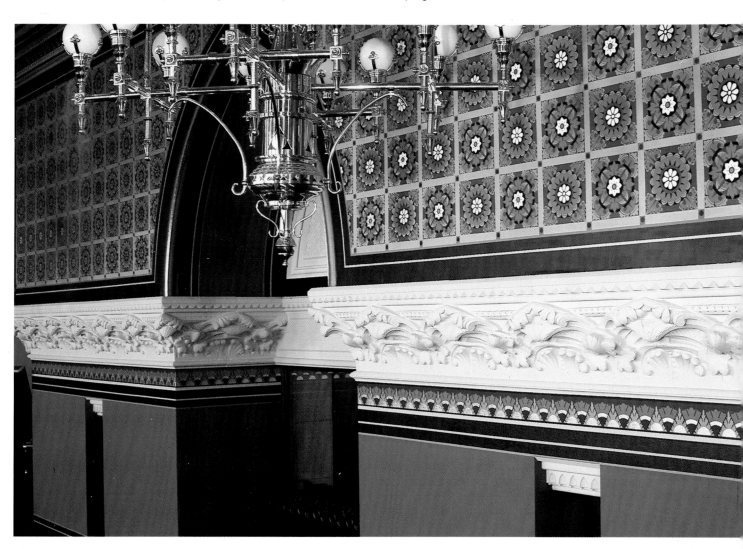

1

2

3

4

5

The rosette patterns for the Chamber ceiling required very special care and attention. The same type of ornament filled the center of each of the six ceiling sections. In this series of photographs, various steps in the re-stenciling of this complicated ornament are illustrated.

1. The general outline of the ornament was properly positioned in the square space. 2. More precise inner lines were stenciled. 3. Various elements were then stencil-painted. 4 and 5. After the chain used to hang a chandelier was affixed and the fixture dropped into place, small elements in the design were hand-painted.

Before and after shots of an upper corner of the Hall of Flags in the Capitol provide striking testimony to the talent of Canning and his assistants. Unlike the radically altered design of the Senate Chamber, William McPherson's late-1870s design for the Hall of Flags had remained relatively undisturbed for more than a century. But large sections had been overpainted, and the general condition of the still-visible decoration was poor and required very careful cleaning. In many places, new applications of paint and gold leaf were called for. The medallions required special treatment. Layers of yellowed varnish and grime were first removed from these and the other patterns before any repainting could be done. John Canning is shown applying new applications of gold leaf after the cleaning process.

Where necessary, paint was chipped away or softened with alcohol so that it could be removed without damaging the underlying design. Cleaning of all the visible and revealed surfaces confirmed Canning's theory that the original colors were still intact and, in many areas, would require only retouching.

John Canning is shown inspecting a medallion before its cleaning and repainting. A simple device extended from the medallion's exact center served to guide his hand when retouching an outer border.

Once all the surfaces were renewed, they were covered with a treatment of acrylic varnish guaranteed not to yellow over time. It is also a finish that can be removed at some future date without damaging the stencil or hand-painted work. One of Canning's restoration precepts is "Never do anything that cannot be reversed."

Ancient Crafts Updated

The former Middlesex County Courthouse complex in East Cambridge, Massachusetts, was converted in 1984 for commercial office space, a restaurant, gallery, theater, and offices for arts and cultural organizations. Renamed Bulfinch Square in honor of the architect, Charles Bulfinch, who designed the central block in 1814, the project was undertaken by Graham Gund Associates of Boston. Reza Jahedi was responsible for the restoration of all historic finishes, but concentrated primarily on the reworking of the Old Superior Courthouse courtroom ceiling, shown opposite and in a detail, below. The restoration scheme returned the ceiling and frieze to their 1901 state, restoring colors to their former brilliance, and repairing the plaster where necessary. The textured mosaic patterning of the ceiling panels and the decoration of the enormous center rosette-ventilator were rendered in an arabesque style with which Jahedi is thoroughly familiar.

The prosaic name "ARJ Associates" says little about either the firm's work or its principal. Behind the letters, however, stands a highly distinct individual—Ali Reza Jahedi. Iranian by birth, trained and employed in his native land and in England in architectural painting and fine art conservation, he is one of the most talented craftsmen working in North America today. Jahedi began his work in the Boston area in 1981 after serving as an associate with British designer John Cairns in London for two years. Prior to that time and the Iranian cultural revolution which brought an end to most preservation projects in that country, he gained a deep knowledge of restoration techniques and traditional finishes. While working on ancient monuments dating back in time to 400 B.C., Jahedi mastered the antique crafts of stenciling, tile design, marbleizing and glazing, and decorative plasterwork—all practiced in the Persian empire when Europe was still in the shadow of civilization and the Western hemisphere was but a figment of the imagination.

Jahedi was attracted to Boston, the most traditional of American cities, because of its long-time commitment to honor and preserve the architectural past. Within a year

or two of his arrival, he was restoring plasterwork, re-stenciling ceilings, and repainting walls in private Back Bay mansions and downtown office buildings. In 1984 he accomplished his most important work to date: the restoration of three elaborately painted Renaissance Revival ceilings in the Bulfinch Square/Old Middlesex County Courthouse in East Cambridge. Since that time, Jahedi and his associates have branched out further to New York and Philadelphia, executing contemporary restaurant and residential designs.

The ceiling side panels and square sub-panels in the old courtroom of the Bulfinch Square contain a densely patterned mosaic design. This has been painted in a light brown and shaded with a darker brown, both colors contrasting handsomely with the sky-blue field of the large center panel. Each of the squares also contains a medallion which is painted gray-brown with the raised foliage painted a dark blue. The ring around each medallion is highlighted in cherry red.

Jahedi's measured drawings of the center and side panels were needed to lay out a color scheme. Altogether, over a dozen colors and shades were applied to the ceiling panels, cornice, and frieze. Certain elements were also outlined in gold leaf. The walls of the courtroom, now used as a concert hall, were painted in a light cream color with accents of brown, orange, and white in the windows and shutters.

A cornice and wide frieze run around all four sides of the space. Both were cleaned and repaired and then given a mottled, soft finish of raw umber against an ocher ground. Jahedi and his assistant "ragged" the beams in the same shades, first brushing them with the ochre glaze and then using a soft cloth to rub in the raw umber.

155

A second room in the Superior Court Building of the Bulfinch Square was adapted for office space. The walls here are divided into two areas above wooden wainscoting. Both were painted in the original tones of gray-green, the moldings being accented in white. A broad cornice ties all four sides of the room together. Above this is a cove ceiling. Jahedi restored all the 1891 colors, a soft palette of cream, light and dark brown, dark green, and gold. Gold leaf was used for the highly decorative guilloche band and the bead-and-reed moldings of the cove.

The ceiling has recessed panels from which four chandeliers are suspended. The same soft colors used in the walls and cove appear here—gray-green, gray, and gray-white for moldings. A circular area around each of the chandeliers was stenciled in a grillwork pattern.

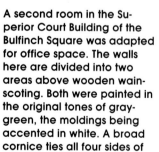

157

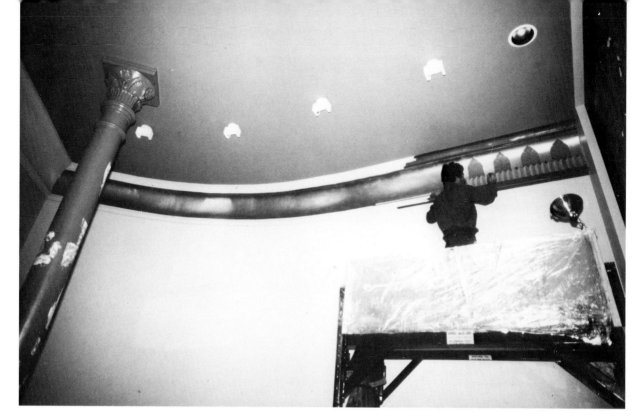

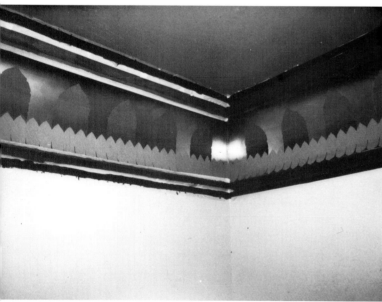

Jahedi is an accomplished stenciler and is shown at work on the entrance lobby of 20 Winthrop Square, Boston. He has researched stencil patterns from ancient Persia to early America and their application to glass, wood, tile, and plaster surfaces. In this project, the designs were stenciled on a gold background in two tones of green.

Among Jahedi's recently completed contemporary design projects is the Cypress Restaurant in Philadelphia. The establishment's name dictated the central decorative motif—a cypress tree made of plaster and painted in two tones of dark blue. Above the tree is a stenciled border in navy blue and gold. The other walls are composed of blocks of *faux* marble.

Expanding the Art of Stenciling

Artist Lynn Goodpasture's quiet, unassuming manner is a most attractive part of her personality, but her sober demeanor cannot hide the equally appealing imaginative and unconventional side of her nature. A stencil artist for the past decade, she is recognized as one of the very best in the field. After graduation from the Corcoran School of Art in Washington, D.C., she became an assistant to Cile Lord, a modern pioneer in the revival of stencil painting. On her own in New York for the past seven years, Goodpasture is frequently called upon by architects and designers, painting studios, and other private clients to execute precise, traditional floral and geometric stencil borders and motifs on walls, ceilings, and floors. So good has she become, indeed, that the apprentice is now the master, a teacher of periodic stenciling classes at New York's Cooper-Hewitt Museum of Decorative Art. Goodpasture is also accomplished in

"Fans," a canvas floorcloth design, is meant to represent a dreamy, sleepy state of mind. Colors drift into each other in a scale ranging from the dark blue of night to the bright reddish-orange of the rising sun. Each of the fans is stencil-painted in a random manner rather than in a traditional repeating pattern. The overall view of the 7' by 5' floorcloth shows how arbitrary and spontaneous the design is.

gold-leaf application, marbleizing, and other painted finishes. However, stenciling traditional motifs is to her, what playing scales would be to a gifted pianist—a fundamental exercise. Fortunately, Goodpasture allows herself flights of fancy in design which carry the art of architectural painting into interesting new dimensions. Her abstract floorcloth designs, many of which have been exhibited at New York's National Craft Showroom, show her to be an innovative and gifted contemporary artist. And they point to a continued career in design and painting full of rich invention.

Somewhat more conventional in approach than the "Fans" design is the "Tropics Floor" motif stenciled on the floor of an entrance hall. The bleached and white-stained surface carries diagonal bands of a stylized leaf pattern broken by figures of elephants, lions, peacocks, and palm trees. An original design by Goodpasture, it was executed in japan paint.

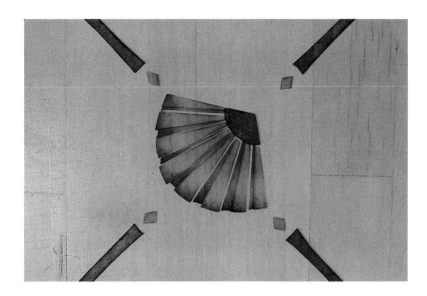

In the bathroom of her own New York loft apartment, Goodpasture has stenciled a simple and elegant design.

Thin diagonal lines hold together randomly placed shell motifs, each of which has been uniquely colored. The oak floor was bleached and stained white before stenciling.

An early twentieth-century Art Nouveau tulip design has been adapted by the artist for another floorcloth. The detail shows a regular repeat pattern; the colors—purples and reds—are randomly distributed. The 6'5'' by 5'5'' rug is enclosed within a subtle diamond border, also stenciled in random colors.

A detail from a geometric floorcloth illustrates the inventive composition which marks much of Goodpasture's contemporary work. The overall design was stenciled on a 7-foot-square piece of heavy cotton canvas, backed with felt, and then given three coats of a scuff-resistant finish. The floorcloth has been exhibited at the National Craft Showroom in New York.

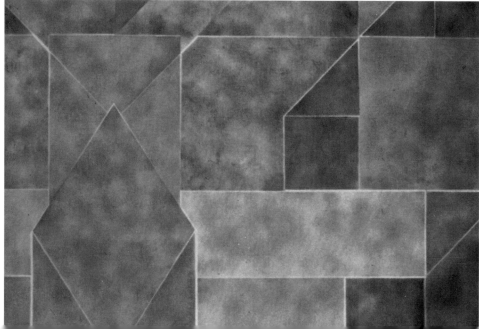

Representative of the traditional designs executed by Goodpasture is one used in a frieze for the Kinterra restaurant in the Wayne Hotel, Wayne, Pennsylvania. The background is a mottled gray glaze upon which an original design in japan paint and gold leaf appears. The dining room ceiling was treated with a blue glaze and given a ragged finish. A crown molding above the frieze was painted with bands of color, including gold-leaf striping.

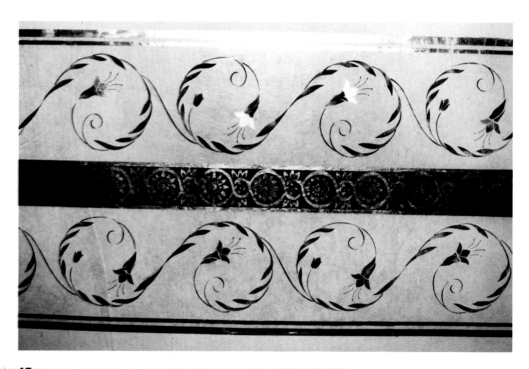

A border in a New York apartment was stenciled on paper and then applied to the ceiling. The design was adapted by Goodpasture from historic documents provided by the architect of the project, Peter Marino. Processes used in the three-part composition included glazing, stenciling, and hand-painting in japan paint and gold leaf. The work was performed on a subcontract basis with EverGreene Studios, the decorating contractor.

David Arky

Lynn Goodpasture calls this design her "Self-Portrait" floorcloth. Measuring 49" by 32", it was created as a demonstration piece for a private floorcloth class held in her studio. The combination of traditional and contemporary motifs reflects her own dual aesthetic interests.

Similar in design to the "Self-Portrait" floorcloth is another model entitled "Fissure." Like the other design, color is used at random within a regular repeating pattern. The gap is an intentional addition. Goodpasture explains that such a visual break adds another dimension of light to the design. The fissure shown in the detail meanders across the design as if to suggest that the artist mismeasured the various components.

Six different traditional patterns were used in the decoration of a bedroom in a private residence in Fairfield, Connecticut. Built in the eighteenth century, the house is an appropriate setting for stenciling in the style of an early itinerant artist. Although regular in pattern, the design has a flow and freedom often missing from period stencil art.

Lynn Goodpasture also designs floorcloths with traditional designs. The basket design appears on a circular rug, the canvas for which was sponged in several colors before the design was stenciled. In color and composition, it has the appearance of nineteenth-century theorem painting. The detail shows the bird perched on a branch in the upper right of the basket.

The dining room in the same Connecticut house has four related stencil patterns filling various wall areas. Stencil art was often used in place of such architectural detail as moldings, and it was appropriate to use painted decoration to form a wall frieze and to surround the fireplace opening.

Beyond Time and Space

Christian Thee is a magician, an artist who conjures up wonderful and surprising images on canvas. Educated as an architect and stage designer, he possesses a superb sense of perspective and drama. If the economics of the Broadway theater were more favorable in the 1980s, he might spend all of his days backstage inventing new and evocative sets, but his theatrical work is now limited to small productions and the annual Spoleto Festival in Charleston, South Carolina, his home town. Rather, he works his theatrical effects to great advantage in residential and commercial settings, drawing primarily on his extraordinary talent for trompe l'oeil painting. Until recently his home and studio was a converted warehouse in Brooklyn Heights, a wonderland of painted architectural decoration. Photographed by *Interior Design*, the English *House and Garden,* Germany's *Ambiente,* and the Italian publication *Brava Casa*, the building achieved a fame which was the envy of interior designers everywhere. But Thee became somewhat bored with it and disillusioned with the neighborhood's rapid commercialization. Home is now a gentlemanly spread in Connecticut's Fairfield County. He is still up to his old painterly tricks, however, and commission after commission pours forth from a recently converted barn/studio. Murals for the Meridien Hotel in New Orleans, painted ceilings to adorn the Buccellati showrooms in New York's Trump Tower, a specially commissioned nine-foot birthday portrait of Prince Andrew, eight trompe l'oeil windows for the Warwick Post Hotel in Houston—these and many other projects keep him very much at center stage in the art world.

Two trompe l'oeil bookcases in the form of hinged screens represent Christian Thee's work at its most witty and exacting. On the opposite page is a tribute to various celebrities from the world of entertainment. Among them is actress Betsy Palmer, whose role as Nora in Henrik Ibsen's *A Doll's House* is symbolized by a scale model of Nora and Torvald Helmer's farmhouse, painted in the upper left shelf. Cole Porter is shown peeping through the second shelf from the top on the right.

The second bookcase-screen, in Victorian style, was a special commission and includes on its shelves books and objects of personal value to the owner.

Thee's mastery of trompe l'oeil painting is captured in this selection of various decorated surfaces. A painted table top (*left*) holds both real and *faux* objects, the pen and sketch being the only painted effects.

The trompe l'oeil window (*opposite page, top*) is one of eight designed for the rotunda of the Lincoln Post Hotel in Houston.

Both left and right sides of the painted closet (shown on the opposite page in its entirety and in a detail) are closed, appearances to the contrary. The panel moldings and the still-life composition, including the suspended yo-yo, are delightful tricks guaranteed to fool the eye.

An extraordinary trompe l'oeil painting with a hidden mechanism to change the scene is illustrated in three different views. First exhibited in Palm Beach, Florida, twelve years ago, it drew the rapt attention of even that blasé audience for which art is a social event and not of aesthetic value in itself. The painting is now part of the collection of the Flint Institute of Art in Michigan.

When a motor built into the window sill is turned on, the shutters stay open approximately two minutes, revealing the birdcage and cat.

Closed momentarily, the shutters then open once again to suggest that the right-hand sash has opened and that the cat is in pursuit of the formerly caged bird. Only the panel-sash has indeed changed. This magic is achieved through the use of a magnetic electronic device which flips a panel painted on both sides.

As the artist himself explains, Thee is always attempting to appeal "to the child" in the viewer. And he readily admits that it is the child within him that calls forth such delightful visual games.

It is sometimes difficult to decide which side of a trompe l'oeil screen created by Thee to exhibit. He insists on painting both front and back with trompe l'oeil motifs. Owner Frederick Koch prefers this rear view, although innocent visitors to his apartment have been overheard muttering about the seeming incongruity.

SELECTED LIST OF ARCHITECTURAL PAINTERS WORKING IN THE UNITED STATES

Tish and John Albright
400 Rodman Avenue
Jenkintown, Pennsylvania 19046
(215) 887-3087

See chapter 15.

ARJ Associates
310 Washington Street
Brighton, Massachusetts 02135
(617) 783-0467

See chapter 18.

Artistic License in San Francisco
855 Alverdo
San Francisco, California 94108
(415) 285-4544

A guild of artisans specializing in all phases of Victorian decoration.

Garth Benton
P.O. Box 1064
Pebble Beach, California 93953
(408) 372-7457

A world-famous painter of murals, including recently completed work for the J. Paul Getty Museum in Malibu, California.

Biltmore, Campbell, Smith Restorations, Inc.
1 Biltmore Plaza
Asheville, North Carolina 28803
(704) 274-1776

See chapter 14.

Eloi Bordelon
308 East 79th Street
New York, New York 10021
(212) 249-9692

An interior designer and mural painter whose recent work includes the sky ceiling in New York's St. Regis Hotel.

Larry Boyce & Associates
Box 421507
San Francisco, California 94142
(415) 626-2122

See chapter 5.

Bob Buckter
3877 20th Street
San Francisco, California 94114
(415) 922-7444

A color consultant and contractor who concentrates primarily on exterior work.

Sydney Butchkes
340 East 57th Street
New York, New York 10022
(212) 688-7454

An artist working by commission through interior designers and specializing in contemporary decoration.

John Canning
132 Meeker Road
Southington, Connecticut 06489
(203) 621-2188

See chapter 17.

David Cohn
240 Waverly Place
New York, New York 10014
(212) 741-3548

See chapter 16.

Craftsmen Decorators
2611 Ocean Avenue
Brooklyn, New York 11229
(718) 332-2106

A firm of three experienced, talented artisans—Helmut Buecherl, James Garaghty, and Howard Zucker—who can produce any type of decorative effect.

Crown Restoration
18 Homer Avenue
Cortland, New York 13045
(607) 756-2632

A fine group of craftsmen with an enviable reputation for historically correct restoration work.

George Davis and Bruce Dilts
Box 1403
Nantucket, Massachusetts 02554
(617) 228-9525

Painters who work in a traditional mode strongly influenced by American folk art.

The Day Studio Workshop
1504 Bryant Street
San Francisco, California 94103
(415) 626-9300

See chapter 2.

Designed Communications
704 Boyle Building, 103 West Capitol
Little Rock, Arkansas 72201
(501) 372-2056

See chapter 4.

Hellmuth and Hellgah Dieken
12441 Nedra Drive
Granada Hills, California 91344
(818) 366-8862

See chapter 9.

Envirographics
2326 Third Street, Suite 347
San Francisco, California 94107
(415) 861-1118

The company undertakes the design and development of custom fine-art painting, murals, and finishes. Edwin Chapman, a noted San Francisco muralist, is an associate.

EverGreene Painting Studios
365 West 36th Street
New York, New York 10018
(212) 239-1322

See chapter 12.

David Fisch
1014 South Main Street
Spring Valley, New York 10977
(914) 352-7588

See chapter 3.

A trompe l'oeil mural executed by Envirographics for a fashion boutique in Hawaii.

Pamela Friend
590 King Street
Hanover, Massachusetts 02339
(617) 878-7596

One of the masters of early American stencil decoration.

George Studios
45-04 97 Place
Corona, New York 11368
(718) 271-2506

The firm undertakes hand-painted decoration and fine arts conservation.

Lynn Goodpasture
42 West 17th Street
New York, New York 10011
(212) 989-5246

See chapter 19.

The Grammar of Ornament
2626 Curtis Street
Denver, Colorado 80205
(303) 295-2431

See chapter 6.

A. Greenhalgh & Sons
P.O. Box 400
Chelmsford, Massachusetts 01824
(617) 256-3777

A company devoted primarily to stencil design and painting.

Caryl Hall Studios
143 Main Street
Cold Spring Harbor, New York 11724
(516) 367-8777

See chapter 10.

Jean-Pierre Heim
241 West 36th Street
New York, New York 10036
(212) 239-0776

A French architect and mural painter known for his work in hotels and restaurants.

A. T. Heinsbergen Co.
7415 Beverly Boulevard
Los Angeles, California 90036
(213) 934-1134

This firm was responsible for the design and decoration of many early Los Angeles area movie theaters. It has since participated in their restoration.

Judith Hendershot
1408 Main Street
Evanston, Illinois 60202
(312) 475-6411

See chapter 11.

Robert Jackson
Box 117
Germantown, New York 12526

A fine painter of classical scenes and an expert with faux finishes. He works primarily through decorators.

Patrick Kennedy
17 White Street
New York, New York 10013
(212) 925-1190

An accomplished muralist and painter of faux finishes.

Nancy A. Kintisch
84-66 98th Street
Woodhaven, New York 11421
(718) 849-8308

See chapter 7.

Alan Long
500 West 22nd Street
New York, New York 10010
(212) 691-3325

A painter by avocation, he is skilled at creating exotic finishes and Art Deco and Art Nouveau designs.

Cile Lord
42 East 12th Street
New York, New York 10003
(212) 228-6030

A well-known teacher and practitioner of traditional stencil art.

Terry Marshall
1515 Homeland Avenue
Norman, Oklahoma 73069
(405) 321-3894

Responsible for the restoration of major buildings in the Midwest and Southwest.

Richard Neas
157 East 71st Street
New York, New York 10021
(212) 772-1878

An interior designer, Neas also executes superb trompe l'oeil work.

Sarah Oliphant Studio
38 Cooper Square
New York, New York 10003
(212) 741-1233

A painter of larger than life murals appropriate for commercial and residential installation.

Megan Parry
1727 Spruce Street
Boulder, Colorado 80302
(303) 444-2724

See chapter 13.

Edward K. Perry Co.
322 Newbury Street
Boston, Massachusetts 02115
(617) 536-7873

A well-established decorating firm responsible for major projects such as Colonial Williamsburg, Old Sturbridge Village, and the Winterthur Museum.

The Rambusch Co.
40 West 13th Street
New York, New York 10011
(212) 675-0400

The East Coast's number-one restoration contractor with a staff of highly talented painters and designers.

Malcolm Robson
Robson Worldwide Graining, Ltd.
4308 Argonne Drive
Fairfax, Virginia 22032
(703) 978-5331

One of the most accomplished British craftsmen working in North America. His projects include Mount Vernon, the Philadelphia Athenaeum, and the Gellier House Museum in New Orleans.

Conrad Schmitt Studios
2405 South 162nd Street
New Berlin, Wisconsin 53151
(414) 786-3030

The Midwest's leading restoration contractor with a staff skilled in all painting techniques and finishes.

Lincoln Seligman
Trompe L'Oeil Institute and Gallery
24 East 81st Street
New York, New York 10028
(212) 249-5300

Working primarily out of London, this artist also undertakes ambitious trompe l'oeil projects in the United States.

Kenneth Stern
Barbara Tamerin Fine Arts
120 East 81st Street
New York, New York 10028
(212) 737-6592

A creator of phantasmaoric landscapes.

Virginia Teichner
P.O. Box 844
New Canaan, Connecticut 06840
(203) 966-4863

An artist who divides her time between traditional stenciling projects and those requiring trompe l'oeil illusion.

Christian Thee
49 Old Stagecoach Road
Weston, Connecticut 06883
(203) 454-0340

See chapter 20.

Tromploy Studio and Gallery
400 Lafayette Street
New York, New York 10003
(212) 420-1639

Painted decoration of every sort, including painted furniture, is executed by the members of this studio.

Valley Craftsmen Ltd.
Box 11
Stevenson, Maryland 21153
(301) 484-3891

Faux finishes, gilding, glazing, trompe l'oeil, murals, and Oriental brush painting are the areas mastered by this group of artists.

Tania Vartan
970 Park Avenue
New York, New York 10028
(212) 744-6710

Floral patterns are executed on floors and walls. She works primarily through decorators.

Scott Waterman
266 B Oxford Place N.E.
Atlanta, Georgia 30307
(404) 373-9438

See chapter 1.

David B. Wiggins
Box 420, Hale Road
Tilton, New Hampshire 03276
(603) 286-3046

See chapter 8.

Lorenz Zetlin
248 East 21st Street
New York, New York 10010
(212) 473-3291

An accomplished mural painter who also undertakes trompe l'oeil work and marbleizing.

Four types of *faux* marble finishes used for the floor of a room in a Connecticut home by craftsmen from the Tromploy Studio and Gallery.

The ceiling of the main lobby at the Lord Baltimore Hotel, Baltimore, as painted and glazed by Valley Craftsmen, Ltd. Metal leaf details were also applied in this restoration.

REGIONAL DIRECTORY OF ARCHITECTURAL PAINTERS

Arkansas
Designed Communications

California
Artistic License in San Francisco
Garth Benton
Larry Boyce & Associates
Bob Buckter
The Day Studio Workshop
Hellmuth and Hellgah Dieken
Envirographics
A. T. Heinsbergen

Colorado
The Grammar of Ornament
Megan Parry

Connecticut
John Canning
Virginia Teichner
Christian Thee

Georgia
Scott Waterman

Illinois
Judith Hendershot

Maryland
Valley Craftsmen

Massachusetts
ARJ Associates
George Davis and Bruce Dilts
Pamela Friend
A. Greenhalgh & Sons
Edward K. Perry Co.

New Hampshire
David Wiggins

New York
Eloi Bordelon
Sydney Butchkes
David Cohn
Craftsmen Decorators
Crown Restoration
EverGreene Painting Studios
David Fisch
George Studios
Lynn Goodpasture
Caryl Hall Studios
Jean-Pierre Heim
Robert Jackson
Patrick Kennedy
Nancy Kintisch
Alan Long
Cile Lord
Richard Neas
Sarah Oliphant Studio
The Rambusch Co.
Lincoln Seligman
Kenneth Stern
Tromploy Studio and Gallery
Tania Vartan
Lorenz Zetlin

North Carolina
Biltmore, Campbell, Smith
  Restorations

Oklahoma
Terry Marshall

Pennsylvania
Tish and John Albright

Virginia
Robson Worldwide Graining

BIBLIOGRAPHY

A few of the titles listed below may not be in print at the present time. It is more than likely, however, that they can be found in public library collections.

Albers, Josef. *Interaction of Color*. rev. ed. New Haven, Ct.: Yale University Press, 1975.

Allen, Edward B. *Early American Wall Paintings 1710-1850*. 1926. Reprint. Library of American Art Series. New York: Da Capo Press, 1971.

Bishop, Adele, and Cile Lord. *The Art of Decorative Stenciling*. New York: Penguin, 1978.

Blake, Wendon. *The Acrylic Painting Book*. New York: Watson-Guptill Publications, 1978.

Cerwinske, Laura. *Tropical Deco: The Architecture and Design of Old Miami Beach*. New York: Rizzoli, 1981.

Cobb, Hubbard H. *How to Paint Anything*. New York: Macmillan, 1974.

De Grandis, Luigina. *Theory and Use of Color*. New York: Harry N. Abrams, 1986.

Dresser, Christopher. *Art of Decorative Design*. Library of Victorian Culture Series. Watkins Glen, N.Y.: American Life Foundation, 1977.

_____. *Modern Ornamentation*. 1862. Reprint. Edited by Peter Stansky and Rodney Shewan. Vol. 26 of Aesthetic Movement and the Arts and Crafts Movement Series. New York: Garland Publishing, 1978.

Eastlake, Charles L. *Hints on Household Taste in Furniture, Upholstery, and Other Details*. 1878. Reprint. Mineola, N.Y.: Dover Publications, 1969.

Finch, Christopher. *Special Effects: Creating Movie Magic*. New York: Abbeville Press, 1986.

Frankenstein, Alfred. *The Reality of Appearance: The Trompe L'Oeil Tradition in American Painting*. New York: New York Graphic Society, 1970.

Grow, Lawrence, and Dina Von Zweck. *American Victorian: A Style and Source Book*. New York: Harper & Row, Publishers, 1984.

Haas, Richard. *Richard Haas: An Architecture of Illusion*. New York: Rizzoli, 1982.

Hemming, Charles. *Paint Finishes*. Secaucus, N. J.: Chartwell Books, 1985.

Innes, Jocasta. *Paint Magic: The Home Decorator's Guide to Painted Finishes*. New York: Van Nostrand Reinhold Company, 1981.

Jencks, Charles. *The Language of Post-Modern Architecture*. 4th rev. ed. New York: Rizzoli, 1984.

Jewett, Kenneth, and Stephen Whitney. *Early New England Wall Stencils*. New York: Harmony Books, 1979.

Jones, Owen. *The Grammar of Ornament*. 1856. Reprint. New York: Van Nostrand Reinhold Company, 1982.

Lacquer: An International History and Illustrated Survey. New York: Harry N. Abrams, 1984.

Little, Nina Fletcher. *American Decorative Wall Painting*. New York: E. P. Dutton, 1972.

_____. *Country Arts in Early American Homes*. New York: E. P. Dutton, 1975.

Mayer, Ralph. *The Artist's Handbook of Materials and Techniques*. 4th rev. ed. New York: Viking Press, 1981.

Mejetta, Mirko, and Simonetta Simon. *Creating Interiors for Unusual Spaces: Designs from Around the World*. Translated by Meg Shore. New York: Watson-Guptill Publications, 1984.

Milman, Miriam. *Trompe-L'Oeil Painting: The Illusion of Reality*. New York, Rizzoli, Skira, 1983.

O'Neil, Isabel. *The Art of the Painted Finish for Furniture & Decoration: Antiquing, Lacquering, Gilding & The Great Impersonators*. New York: Quill, 1980.

Parry, John P. *Parry's Graining and Marbling.* 2d ed. Revised by Brian Rhodes and John Windsor. Dobbs Ferry, N.Y.: Sheridan House, 1985.

Parry, Megan. *Stenciling.* New York: Van Nostrand Reinhold Company, 1982.

Porter, Tom. *Architectural Color: A Design to Using Color on Buildings.* New York: Watson-Guptill Publications, Whitney Library of Design, 1985.

Radford, Penny. *Designer's Guide to Surfaces and Finishes.* New York: Watson-Guptill Publications, Whitney Library of Design, 1984.

Seale, William. *Recreating the Historic House Interior.* Nashville, Tenn.: American Association for State and Local History, 1979.

Street-Porter, Tim. *L. A. Houses.* New York: Stewart, Tabori & Chang, 1986.

Waring, Janet. *Early American Stencils on Walls and Furniture.* Mineola, N.Y.: Dover Publications, 1937.

Wharton, Edith, and Ogden Codman, Jr. *The Decoration of Houses.* 1902. Reprint. New York: W.W. Norton & Company, 1978.

Wilcox, Michael. *Color Theory for Oil Colors or Acrylics.* New York: Watson-Guptill Publications, 1983.

INDEX